The Charismatic

Ministry

Gordon Lindsay

Published By
CHRIST FOR THE NATIONS, INC.
Dallas, Texas
Reprint 1983

CONTENTS

CHAPTER 1

The Call of God

"But ye are a chosen generation, a royal priesthood, an holy nation, a peculiar people; that ye should shew forth the praises of him who hath called you out of darkness into his marvellous light" (1 Peter 2:9).

In a sense every believer is called to be a follower of Christ and a witness for Him. The Lord Jesus worked in the carpenter shop before He preached the gospel. Whatever a man does, whether he is called to work with his hands or otherwise, he should do it as unto the Lord. But beyond working with his hands, God calls every man to some spiritual service. The church being the body of Christ has many members. It is intended that all shall contribute in some way to the edification of the body. There are those who minister in the gifts of the Spirit. Some are called to be teachers, youth workers, or personal workers. Others have special talents in counseling. Still others may have a ministry in music or song. All should have a ministry of prayer.

Beyond these callings there is a distinctive ministry in which a man is divinely appointed to the preaching of the gospel. As Paul says in Romans 10:15, "And how shall they preach, except they be sent?" Jesus called certain disciples and prepared them for the work of the ministry. The calling of Peter and Andrew and the two Zebedee sons is an example (Matt. 4:18-22). The call of God to the ministry is a real and definite thing.

How can a man know he is called to the ministry? The initiative comes from God. "No man taketh this honor unto himself" (Heb. 5:4). A man does not plan to become a minister as he would decide to choose one of the secular professions. Often, though not always, the call is associated with a powerful spiritual experience. Perhaps the last thing in the world the man would have chosen would be the ministry, but after the Spirit of God moved upon his heart and changed his life, he suddenly found himself eagerly desiring that in which he once had no interest.

The question the man must ask himself in determining the

3

reality of his calling to the ministry is whether or not he has an overwhelming concern for the souls of men and women. Would he be ready to sacrifice, to put himself out for them? Can he share and understand their petty concerns? Unless he can love people as they are, feel for them, sympathize with them, and carry their burdens, he is not likely to induce them to be concerned with the things pertaining to God's kingdom.

Sometimes friends can tell if a man is called to the ministry. But they are not always right, nor are they always in a position to know how God may be dealing with a man. Some of the church's greatest soul-winners were discouraged by others from entering the ministry. For instance, one of the world's leading denominational evangelists was rejected by a young lady whom he was courting because she didn't believe he had "what it took" to succeed in the ministry. Nevertheless, this caution may be considered a test. When Elisha prayed Elijah that he might follow in his ministry, Elijah replied, "Thou hast asked a hard thing." Elisha, as we know, did pass the test. The criterion of a God-called minister that Jesus gave to His followers is this: "If any man will come after me, let him deny himself and take up his cross and follow me" (Matt. 16:24).

In the final analysis the person himself must decide whether or not he has the courage and fortitude to persevere against all obstacles that he must face if he enters the ministry. For one thing he can test himself by his faithfulness to his home church. If he is not loyal to it, how can he expect others to be loyal to him? Candidates for the ministry have ample opportunity to prove themselves in their own assemblies by their faithful attendance, by assisting in the young people's work, in house-to-house visitation, in their giving, in whatever duties the pastor assigns to them. Others will assess a man by his faithfulness in carrying out the tasks given him in the local church. If in their opinion a young man's actions show him to be unstable and undependable, he may well question his call to the ministry.

It has been well said that if a man can be happy in any other vocation than the ministry, he can be sure he is not called. Certainly the call must be a compelling one. Can the man say as Paul, "Necessity is laid upon me"? As he looks out into the state of the world, does his calling grip him so strongly that he can follow no other course? Does it hold a real challenge to him? Does it kindle in him a flame, a passion, that no obstacle, no disappointment can crush or erase from his soul? Does the call

4

get such a hold on him that he is willing to spend hours in prayer?

It is well that these questions be answered before a man commits himself. There is nothing attractive about a man's entering the ministry and finding himself a misfit. The ministry is an exacting occupation. But he who knows his calling is truly of God and toils on, rising above all disappointments, knowing that in the end the Master will say, "He that is faithful in that which is least is faithful also in much," will surely find success.

What should be a man's first step when he is called to the ministry? The moment one feels called is the time to begin preparation. This should never cease. The need of study and preparation is clearly set forth in II Timothy 2:15: "Study to shew thyself approved unto God, a workman that needeth not to be ashamed, rightly dividing the word of truth."

We are living in a time when emphasis is being placed on education as a necessary preparation for any profession. Although the ministry is more than a profession, a well-trained minister has a far wider field of usefulness than one who has a limited education. It is to be noted that an ever-increasing proportion of high-school graduates now go to college. The training of one's mind gives it accuracy and preciseness of thought. It is significant that when God chose a man to write most of the epistles of the New Testament, He selected Paul who had one of the best educations of his time.

Those who would teach must first be willing to be taught. Moses received a secular education while living in the palace of Pharaoh. Afterwards he received further instruction on the back side of the desert. When it came time for Joshua to take command, Moses laid his hands upon him that the Spirit of wisdom might be given him. This supernatural gift, however, was not to take the place of personal study. God commanded Joshua to meditate on the Scriptures day and night:

> "This book of the law shall not depart out of thy mouth; but thou shalt meditate therein day and night, that thou mayest observe to do according to all that is written therein: for then thou shalt make thy way prosperous, and then thou shalt have good success" (Josh. 1:8).

From the book of Samuel we gather that this great leader established a school of the prophets (I Sam. 10:5). Elisha in his day encouraged the expansion of this institution. He dwelt with the sons of the prophets and no doubt taught them personally (II Kings 6:1-3). The psalmist declared that the way of a man

5

who delights himself day and night in the Word of the Lord shall be prosperous (Psa. 1:1-3).

Jesus as a boy was found with the doctors of the law "both hearing them and asking questions" (Luke 2:46).

God has put teachers in the church as one of the ministry-gifts (I Cor. 12:28; Eph. 4:11-14). Young men who feel the call to enter the ministry should secure the benefit of the teachings of divinely appointed members of the body of Christ. Some men through spiritual pride reject God's means of instruction. As a consequence they have gone off the deep end and have become the victims of the grossest delusions.

The apostle Peter admonished us to be ready to give an answer to all those who ask for a reason of the hope that is within us (I Pet. 3:15). Certainly diligent study is a prerequisite to a successful ministry.

A mere intellectual knowledge of the Scriptures however is not a sufficient qualification for the ministry. There must be a real experience with God. Nicodemus, a ruler of the Jews, learned in ecclesiastical ritual, knew nothing of the born-again experience. When he asked Jesus, "How can these things be?" the Lord reproached him saying, "Art thou a master of Israel, and knowest not these things?"

It is a solemn fact that thousands of ministers, although they have had formal theological training, have never had a real born-again experience. These men usually build their sermons *around book reviews, current events, sociology, philosophy,* psychology and politics, instead of around the Word of God. Unconverted preachers will preach to unconverted congregations. While it is good for a man who makes the ministry his life's work to have the best possible education, it goes for naught if it is not Spirit-oriented. A minister must not only have an educated mind but an educated heart.

The institution in which a man chooses to get his education can make or break him. He can come out of the school a professionalist, a zealot who argues religion or he can be a trained ambassador of Christ who has a passion for souls. Much depends on whether during his school years he carefully cultivates his spiritual life. Many students out of seminaries are sophisticated intellectuals who have much in their minds but little in their hearts. They go out into the world utterly unprepared to cope with the serious problems of men. But with the Twelve it was not so. Even their enemies "took knowledge of them that they had been with Jesus." A personal acquaintance with Christ is a *must* for a man who would preach the gospel.

CHAPTER 2

Some Qualifications for the Ministry

It is a glorious thing to receive a call to the ministry. There is a majesty about the task of being an ambassador for Almighty God. Yet as a calling the ministry demands certain qualifications. No man is ready to be an effective minister at the time of his call; therefore, he should lose no time in beginning his preparation.

It goes without saying that first of all, his experience of conversion must be deep and real. The unregenerate heart is unable to receive and understand spiritual things, much less instruct others in them. A man by reason of his personal charm and natural abilities may be able to satisfy the religious instincts of a congregation, but without a real experience himself, he is a "blind leader of the blind." Let every man who feels a call to the ministry, therefore, dig down deeply until he is firmly upon the Rock. While Jesus regarded His disciples as saved men (Luke 10:17-20), He did not consider their experience as yet complete. This is clearly seen in Jesus' words to Peter just before the great denial: "And the Lord said, Simon, Simon, behold, Satan hath desired to have you, that he may sift you as wheat: But I have prayed for thee, that thy faith fail not: and *when thou art converted,* strengthen thy brethren" (Luke 22:31-32).

A minister should have a deep sense of the meaning of his conversion. He should ever keep in mind that he has been dug out of the pit and that he has a debt that he can never fully repay. While in his inner life he will have that peace and confidence that comes from resting in Christ, at the same time he will be constantly aware of the dangers and temptations that may confront him—even as the apostle said, "But I keep under my body, and bring it into subjection: lest that by any means, when I have preached to others, I myself should be a castaway" (1 Cor. 9:27).

A minister should certainly have the baptism of the Spirit. Jesus told His disciples that they were not to depart from Jerusalem but to wait for the promise of the Father. He said, "Ye shall receive

7

power, after that the Holy Ghost is come upon you: and ye shall be witnesses unto me both in Jerusalem, and in all Judea, and in Samaria, and unto the uttermost parts of the earth" (Acts 1:8). Since it was a requirement even of deacons to receive the Holy Ghost, it is obvious that ministers of the Word should be filled with the Spirit (Acts 6:3).

The work of the Lord requires everything a man has. There may come a time when a young minister seriously wonders whether he can ever successfully fulfill the demands of the ministry as he senses the enormity of the task before him. When Moses received the call at the Burning Bush, he was in utter despair of his ability to measure up. It seemed humanly impossible as far as he was concerned. Isaiah, startled by the vision of glory when God called him, cried out saying, "Woe is me! for I am undone." Amos declared he was not a prophet nor the son of a prophet, but he obeyed the call and delivered his message to those of his generation.

Although the calling is high and holy, there are usually many obstacles in the way of him who would be a minister of God. It does not eliminate the bafflements that confront everyone who seeks to enter into a chosen life work. The demands that are thrust upon the minister are complex and often bewildering. On Sunday he must preach two fresh and inspiring messages, not including usually teaching an adult class. By disposition he must always appear radiant and buoyant. Among men he must be a man; he must also lend a sympathetic ear to distraught women; he should be able to reach the hearts of little children; he needs the organizing genius necessary to the management of a church; still again he must be able to balance the budget.

This list of requirements is by no means all. If he expects to stay long in his pastorate, he must give time to study and meditation, so that his preaching will not be repetitious. He must be a leader and stay ahead of his congregation. In the parlance of the athletic field, he must carry the ball. If he does not, he will soon find that someone else will, a circumstance that by no means will work to his advantage. At times the task may seem insuperable, but taking courage, he must say as the apostle Paul, "I can do all things through Christ which strengtheneth me" (Phil. 4:13). The secret of the ministry lies in believing this.

A minister must be alert so that he will not lose his perspective as some do. Blinded by the cares of life, he becomes as Samson, "grinding at the mill." The joy and glory of the early morning is gone. He has somehow lost his first love. To such Jesus spoke

8

in His message to the church at Ephesus, "I know thy works, and thy labor, and thy patience . . . and hast borne, and hast patience, and for my name's sake hast labored, and hast not fainted. Nevertheless, I have somewhat against thee, because thou hast left thy first love: (Rev. 2:2-4). A minister must have an unwearying love for people and a devotion to their needs. When that love dims under the stress and strain of daily work, he becomes devitalized. God help a preacher always to retain the spiritual glow! And this can only be achieved by constantly believing.

It is human nature for people to stratify into different social levels. There are some who are naturally more congenial than others. But if ministers subordinate the interests of the poorer and less privileged to those whom they like best, they will let the race of men go by. What made David Livingstone great? Was it not because he left behind him the pleasures and comforts of home and friends to make his lot on the Dark Continent? When he died, the natives cried as children in their great love for this man of God, and they carried his body a thousand miles so that it could be sent back to England to rest in Westminister Abbey.

What are the qualifications for the ministry? If we would help people, we must be patient with them. Many cannot solve their own problems. The underprivileged are often victims of a background that causes them to be slow in grasping truths that are self-evident to others. All need a sympathetic understanding of their problems. One must learn to relate to people and their needs. If one does not learn to help them in their extremity, they will turn to secular counselors, or worse to religious quacks and mountebanks.

The young minister must thoroughly assess what he is up against. The world today is strongly pre-conditioned against spiritual religion. Critics have attacked the inspiration and authenticity of the Scriptures; communism has made a frontal attack against it. Science has raised doubts about the Genesis account. Modern psychology seeks to take the place religion once had. He who would be a successful ambassador of Christ must have more than natural ability; he must have the very power of the supernatural.

The man who would minister effectively today must understand the times in which he is living. He must realize that the very structure of civilization is being shaken, that there is a gigantic struggle that is laying bare the foundations of society. The world is sick, very sick. The minister must go to the heart of the trouble. How can he answer his conscience if he preaches on irrelevancies and does not speak forth on the great issues of life?

The present time is one in which super salesmanship is selling the idea that the chief end of living is obtaining as many of the creature comforts as possible. The newspapers, magazines, radio and television drive this into people's minds continually. The preacher, if he does not watch, will be caught in the same mad whirl of contemporary materialism. What are automobiles, houses, lands, antiques, refrigerators, and television sets when the world around us is breaking up and the shadows of a dying age are reaching out to engulf the souls of men and women in the darkness of eternal night?

What is the message of the hour? Men still need to know that the wages of sin is death, that the judgments of God are in the earth, that souls all around are perishing, that the calling of the preacher is to stand between the living and the dead, that in Christ alone is salvation.

A man must have convictions if he would become a successful minister. He must have backbone. His feet must be planted on the Rock so that he will not be moved. He will not accommodate himself to all manner of pressure groups that would divert his attention from spiritual things or to seek to limit the moving of the Spirit. Always seeking to creep into the church unawares is the leaven of skepticism that would weaken the pillars of Christianity. Is Christ the Son of God indeed? Are the Scriptures the inspired Word of God? Is the story of creation true? Are the miracles of the Bible real? Are the gifts of the Spirit for operation today? A minister cannot be wishy-washy on these things. He must not only know where he stands but be able to defend intelligently the truth which he believes. As Peter said, we should be ready always to give a "reason of the hope that is in us."

There is today an army of ill-assorted preachers who run about over the country championing this and that and the other cause. They want to crusade for something, but know not what. It was because the apostles had a cause they believed in that Christianity experienced its rapid expansion. The minister who has no deep convictions will flop around and drift with the tide. The central truth of the gospel is that Jesus died to save sinners and that the signs of the gospel will follow them that believe. That message must be delivered to mankind.

A man who would be a worthy minister must have compassion. He must not only think clearly, but he must feel deeply. He must feel for his brethren who are toiling and struggling in the world of insecurity. He must relate the gospel to the practical side of living.

He cannot always keep his head in the clouds, but he must come down to earth and be able to say, "I sat where they sat." The minister must be approachable. He must be able to share the common lot. Like Jesus he must have compassion for the multitude and be touched by their infirmities. It is not enough for a minister to live a comfortable life, isolated from the world's miseries; he must come down out of his ivory tower and mingle with the people, feel with them in their pitiful illusions, be willing to defend the weak against injustice and raise a voice against intolerance and prejudice.

The minister above all things must develop character. He must be the soul of integrity. Truth is his shield and buckler. There is no place for the man, regardless of his talents, who is loose in morals. Moreover, he should live simply and not ostentatiously. There are those who in order to keep up a front, spend lavishly, incur debts beyond their ability to pay, and use their credit to the breaking point. What little good they do is cancelled by their careless living. They become a reproach to the ministry rather than a blessing.

We place a high value on the gifts of the Spirit, and this is right. Nevertheless, the gifts without the fruits are as the apostle said, "as sounding brass or a tinkling cymbal." God becomes real to humanity as He is incarnated in holy men and women. Christianity is not so much a religion as it is the life of Christ indwelling the individual. When there is a sharp contradiction between the words one speaks and the life he leads, the net result is zero. Indeed, it can be less than zero. Such a person can actually do injury to the cause of Christ.

As we have said, a minister should never cease learning. A young man preparing for the ministry must first become familiar with the great redemption themes. But he also needs training in practical matters. He should know how to do personal work, how souls are led to Christ, how a church is organized, how an effective youth work is built, how one develops good public relations, how to be tactful yet honest with people, and how to counsel with them. *And crowning all this, he needs the power of God by which he can deliver people from the oppression and snares of Satan. He must have a definite part in apostolic ministry.*

And finally a matter which is so common a subject of conversation these days—the material rewards. This is the time of the affluent society, the age when success is measured in material gain, with the rich getting richer and the poor rising up and

11

demanding their share, by lawful means, or by violence. The question was one that Peter asked Jesus in Mk. 10:28 when he said: "Lo we have left all and have followed thee." They had just witnessed the departure of the rich young ruler, who went back to his riches and Peter was asking what he and his brethren would receive in a material way. Jesus turned to him and made a remarkable statement: Mk. 10:29-30, "And Jesus answered and said, Verily I say unto you, There is no man that hath left house, or brethren, or sisters, or father, or mother, or wife, or children, or lands, for my sake, and the gospel's. But he shall receive an hundredfold now in this time, houses, and brethren, and sisters, and mother, and children, and lands, with persecutions; and in the world to come eternal life."

Can this be possibly true? An hundred fold now in this time? It seems incredible unless you read the conditions carefully. *This promise is for the man who leaves all for the gospel's sake without thought of any return.* He preaches the gospel for the sheer joy of having a place in the harvest field.

As a personal testimony may I say that I was called to preach at a time that I think was just right. I had little training for the ministry and had to learn what I did painfully, little by little. Consequently, I did not expect the people to give me much for my preaching. When I finally got to the place that I thought I had some ministry, the Great Depression came on. People were in such financial straits that there was no use to even hope for an offering that would supply more than the most minimum needs. Preachers shared the poverty of the people. But the day came when God gave abundance. It has been our great joy for years to send substantial help to mission fields of some sixty nations. The desire for luxuries and material things hold no part in our lives. But surely the above promise has proved true in our lives. It will prove true for those who meet the conditions.

CHAPTER 3

The Art of Understanding People

Before we enter into the various phases of the Pentecostal ministry, there is a matter that needs consideration because a shortcoming here can mean failure elsewhere. We refer to a minister's capacity to understand people, to work with them, and to get along with them. This ability is necessary in the realm of the ministry as in any other profession.

To get along with people does not mean that a man has to compromise his principles. Indeed, if he does that, in the end he will probably lose favor with both God and man. But he must be able to win people's confidence before he can help them. We once knew a minister who had unusual faith for miracles, and by reason of this was quickly voted in as pastor of a church. But because of his utter disregard of the principles of human relations, he ultimately failed.

Every young minister should give the subject his most earnest attention. For if he has not learned the art of getting along with people, he will be doomed to mediocrity no matter what his other gifts are. Indeed it is possible that he may never really understand the reason for his lack of success.

The gospel is good news, the greatest story ever told, the most wonderful thing that ever happened to this world. Yet it has to be sold anew to every generation, to every individual. It is a fact that the interest of the average person in his church is determined largely by his feelings toward his pastor. A minister's success, therefore, to a large degree depends upon his ability to produce in his people the feeling that he is worthy of the position he holds as their shepherd. If they come to the conclusion that he is unworthy, his effectiveness as a pastor ceases. This situation may arise, not because he is an unconsecrated man nor because he does not have ability, but simply because he is unable to sell himself to the people. He has failed in the field of public relations.

A minister's inability to function well with people is often caused by certain peculiar habits and personality quirks which are usually possible for him to correct. An unwillingness to try to correct them is a far more serious matter than the faults themselves. Pride may stand in the way of his admitting he is guilty of any fault, and thus he may limit his effectiveness in the ministry or doom himself to mediocrity.

The call to the ministry is a matter between God and the man. But as a noted minister has said, "As he takes up the ministry, however, the issue is no longer between him and God alone, nor is it to be settled in the realm of personal character and energy. He is now to deal with people; and unless he can win and lead those people, his consecration and preparation become abortive." How important is every act of the minister—especially when he begins his labors in a new place and people are forming their opinion of him. How discouraging it is when he learns that the people as a whole have not received him.

What is wrong when a pastor fails to sell himself to his people? Perhaps the most common reason lies in the lack of tact and kindness. There are various things that cause ministers to fail: laziness incompetency, ineffectiveness in the pulpit, but one of the greatest causes of failure is the lack of thoughtfulness or tact. Many ministers have possessed every qualification for service except this one. And why do they lack it? It is largely because they have not taken time to master it. Tact is thoughtfulness of others; it is sensitivity to the atmosphere of the moment; it is a combination of interest, sincerity, and brotherly love—giving the other fellow a sense of ease in one's presence. In a word, it is Christian love—the practice of the golden rule.

It is important for the minister to have good relations, not only with his congregation, but as far as possible with those outside his parish. The opinion others hold of him will be the opinion they hold of his church. This is something of which not all ministers are aware. Indirectly he is always witnessing for Christ and for the church. This outer influence is something that a sensible minister cannot ignore. As a community figure he can lend his influence for God and righteousness far outside the pale of his own congregation.

Yet with the opportunity, there are dangers. A minister in his effort to show that he is human or "one of the boys" can secularize his ministry so that people think of him as a toastmaster, or a man who can tell good stories, or play a fair game of golf. Such a man, even if his life is above reproach can come to be looked

14

upon as a "hail-fellow-well met," but not as a man they want to go to when they need God or when sorrow or tragedy strikes.

That man has unwittingly, perhaps defeated the very purpose of his calling—to lead people to God. Instinctively a man of God should be sensitive to any situation in which good taste is being violated and which he in good conscience cannot endorse or in which he cannot participate. Christ mingled with sinners, but He never temporized with evil nor winked at it. His very presence brought conviction of sin and caused those who came near Him to want to live different lives.

It is well for a minister to establish relations with community leaders. The good will of the officials of the city is invaluable. It also strengthens the pastor with his own people. Such cooperation is usually welcomed by civic leaders. While it is a snare and a delusion for anyone to think that he can reform the whole world, the church should exercise its influence to improve the moral tone of the community. "Ye are the salt of the earth," Jesus said, "but if the salt has lost its savour, wherewith shall it be salted?"

A minister who is active in his community may be asked to join various organizations. He may be requested to lend his name to such movements as Community Chest or Red Cross drives, Parent Teachers' Associations, etc. Some of these organizations he can safely join. There are other types of organizations about which a minister should exercise a great deal of thought, before he identifies with them. Although some of their aims may be laudable, it is quite possible that the organization will be classed as radical. A preacher must be careful not to be stamped as a radical, an agitator, an extremist, nor one who is involved in highly controversial political issues. It is doubtful that a minister will help his cause by joining pickets or protest marches. He is not to spearhead every movement that comes along. Rather he is to develop an image in the minds of the people of the community as a man of God whose judgment can be relied upon.

In this chapter we have considered the human side of the ministry. There is also the supernatural side which is of even greater importance. We shall discuss this in the next chapter.

CHAPTER 4

Supernatural or Non-supernatural Ministry?

In this chapter we consider a matter which basically determines the direction of a minister's life. Every man who is called to minister must decide what his attitude will be toward the supernatural ministry. The gospel minus the supernatural is not really the gospel, and without it a minister is poorly equipped indeed to face and overcome opposing spiritual forces.

But here a word of explanation is needed. No one yet has entered into all the possibilities of the supernatural ministry. And any minister who preaches the born-again experience has shared in it to some degree. What is more supernatural than for the Spirit of God to regenerate and change a lost sinner into a child of God! Every preacher who has souls saved under his ministry whether he realizes it or not, is to some degree ministering in the supernatural. This being the case, he might as well not stop there, but go all the way.

The church desperately needs ministers who have heard from heaven. Jesus asked the Pharisees the question, "The baptism of John, was it from heaven, or of men?" (Luke 20:4). The question placed them in an embarrassing position. For reasons which they considered sufficient, they were against this type of ministry. The people believed in the Baptist, and the Pharisees perceived that in contrast they had become the subjects of an unfavorable comparison. This far from pleased them; nevertheless, they knew that if they said John's ministry was of men, a storm of indignation might arise against them that would further jeopardize their standing with the people. Therefore, they gave Jesus no answer.

Today a similar situation exists in the religious field. The gifts of the Spirit are coming back into the church and have attracted wide attention. This has not only produced the Pentecostal movement, but has made substantial inroads into the historic churches. The question is, which side will a man join? Shall he choose the supernatural ministry regardless of ecclesiastical opinion, or will he

16

take what appears to be the safer way and settle for less than in his heart he knows is the right thing to do.

He who seeks an excuse for holding back will not be at loss to find one. For there are those who profess to represent apostolic ministry whose lives are not altogether what they should be. There always have been individuals in every walk of life who are careless in their conduct. The ministry is no exception. For those who bring discredit on the cause, no defense need be offered; although it must be said that ministers who disturb Satan's kingdom with a supernatural ministry are a special target for his attacks. Always the devil is looking and probing for a man's weakness. Moreover, every action is watched, and every move is under scrutiny. Unless the man takes upon him the whole armor of God, he is in serious danger of becoming a victim of the enemy's attacks.

We thank God that there are many godly men and women who believe and practice apostolic ministry and who maintain a high standard of Christian conduct. Nevertheless, the genuineness of this ministry does not stand nor fall upon the success or failure of any man but upon God's immutable Word. If the Scriptures teach anything at all, they affirm that the same command that Christ gave to the Early Church is in force today: "Teaching them to observe all things whatsoever I have commanded you: and lo, I am with you alway, even unto the end of the world" (Matt. 28:20). The theory that there was a ministry for the Early Church and a different one for today has no foundation in the Scriptures.

Some people concede that the Bible teaches an apostolic ministry but express the view that the time of falling away is here; therefore, we are not to look for further revival. But if there is a falling away, this is not God's fault but man's. Jesus in Luke 18:8 asked a significant question: "Nevertheless when the Son of man cometh, shall he find faith on the earth?" It is evident that neither apostasy nor revival is predestined in the plan of God. Man is free to claim the promises of God or to draw back and fail to enter in, just as the children of Israel were free to enter Canaan but chose to remain in the wilderness.

It is true we are living in the time of falling away as predicted by Paul in I Timothy 4:1. Yet the apostles also lived in a day of apostasy. In fact it was that generation that filled up the full measure of iniquity of their race. They first rejected Christ, then rejected the Holy Spirit, thus bringing age-long judgment

17

upon them. *But during that very time there occurred a great revival in the Early Church—a revival that practically resulted in the evangelization of that generation* (Col. 1:23). Prophecy foresees a lukewarm Laodicean Church at the end-time, but it also reveals that there will be a faithful Philadelphian church (Rev. 3:7-13).

Ezekiel 37 shows that at the end-time there will occur a remarkable revival among the people of Israel. God will breathe His Spirit upon Israel's dry bones in such a way as to result in an epochal spiritual awakening. Joel the prophet foresaw that this outpouring of the Spirit was not only to fall upon the house of Israel, but it was to fall "upon all flesh" (Joel 2:28-30).

The fact is that before the end can come the evangelization of the world must be completed. As Jesus said, "And this gospel of the kingdom shall be preached in all the world for a witness to all nations; and then shall the end come" (Matt. 24:14). It was the miracles occurring in the Early Church that were the catalyst that caused the rapid spread of the gospel, and it is the miracle which can implement the rapid evangelization of the nations of the world in this crucial hour. There is not time for long-term evangelization by methods of yester-years. One after another the doors in foreign lands are being closed to missions. Only the preaching of the gospel *with signs following will* adequately meet the situation of the present hour.

God has some particular phase of supernatural ministry for every man that is called of Him. It may be that He will have a special anointing to minister to the sick. Or it could be that God will use him to bring people into the experience of the baptism of the Holy Spirit again. He may be given one or more gifts of the Spirit. Or he may receive faith for a special type of ministry. "But all these worketh that one and the selfsame Spirit, dividing to *every man severally as he will"* (I Cor. 12:11).

CHAPTER 5

The Place of Prayer in a Minister's Life

Success in the ministry, whatever kind God gives to a man, depends on a consistent prayer life. Failure begins when a man lets down in this important phase of the ministry. The Christian walk is a prayer warfare. How much more is this true in the case of those who are actively engaged in preaching the gospel. They become the favorite targets of Satan, and unless bulwarks are built against the enemy, he will surely attack them at their weakest point. This is why Jesus said to His disciples, "Watch and pray lest ye enter into temptation." Peter heard Jesus speak this warning in the Garden of Gethsemane; nevertheless, he dozed off to sleep. By midnight he had denied his Lord three times.

If Christ felt it necessary to maintain a strong prayer life, how much more His disciples. With the Lord as our example, it would appear that no minister would let down on prayer which is such an important factor to his success. And yet it is true that many ministers gradually cease to have an effective prayer life. They allow themselves to get involved in too many matters, things not necessarily wrong in themselves, except that they take up so much of their time they lose the spirit of prayer. Then little by little the enemy moves in, and before a man knows it, Satan has secured an advantage.

The minister is engaged in a continuous warfare against the powers of darkness. He must never forget this. Paul in Ephesians 6:12 speaks of that warfare in the following powerful language:

> "For we wrestle not against flesh and blood, but against principalities, against powers, against the rulers of the darkness of this world, against spiritual wickedness in high places."

Hebrews 5:7 shows the importance prayer meant to Christ: "Who in the days of his flesh, when he had offered up prayers and supplications with strong crying and tears unto him that was able to save him from death, and was heard in that he feared."

19

Here is surely a vital key to a strong and positive life. *If a minister will maintain an effective prayer life, he will anticipate and prevent many of the ills that would otherwise overtake him.*

While there is more than one reason that some ministers lose their anointing, the most usual of all is that they allow their praying to taper off. Admittedly prayer is a labor. Sometimes it can be a wearisome one. On occasion when one is on his knees, it may seem that time is wasting. But no greater mistake can be made. Prayer brings into action the power of the Infinite, and it sets it to moving on the intercessor's behalf.

It may have seemed to Daniel, when many days had passed, that his praying was in vain (Daniel 10). But not so; when finally the angel of God reached him, he declared that on the first day of his petition God had dispatched him with the answer, but the Prince of Persia had withstood him 21 days. Obviously when the victory came, it was Daniel's persistent intercession that had made the difference.

Consistent prayer builds bulwarks around the believer against the works of darkness. The enemy's sword is blunted. His secret plans for mischief are overruled. The cunning traps he sets are unsprung. A praying man may pass by many dangers and never be aware of them. All because he prayed! Prayerless Christians whether in the pulpit or in the pew are candidates for the devil's snares.

But prayer must be persistent. There is no place for respite. We have observed ministers who have waited before God in prayer and fasting, accepting no denial, until God answered the cry of their hearts and gave them a special anointing. Soon they were reaching large audiences, and many were being converted to Christ. Then gradually their ministry began to wane. The question is, why did this happen?

Let us note the case of one minister who was being mightily used of God, and whose ministry was reaching thousands. Unfortunately, after a time he began to compare himself with others—as some ministers are prone to do, but which the Scriptures admonishes us not to do (II Cor. 10:12). He saw others doing things that he felt were outdistancing him, and he became dissatisfied. He came to the conclusion that what he lacked was a project. God does call certain ones to carry out special work, but this man evidently without getting the mind of God launched into something beyond his depth. Projects can sometimes be very expensive. The need for finances to keep his project going soon had a crippling effect upon his ministry. He was at wit's end to pay his bills. More and more his attention had to be upon raising money instead of waiting upon God. As a result a slow erosion of his ministry set in. Gradually that special anointing that had made his ministry so in demand was largely lost.

God calls men for different tasks. They should stay by what God has given them to do. When a man is called to be an evangelist, in most cases it is going to require his full attention to keep that special anointing of God upon his life. Moreover, of all men, he becomes the special target of the enemy. As Peter and John, he should set and maintain an hour of prayer (Acts 3:1). He should allow nothing, be it ever so pressing, to interfere with that hour.

Much has been said about prayer and fasting. Jesus after ejecting the epileptic demon which the disciples could not cast out, showed the power of the fast by saying, "This kind can come forth by nothing, but by prayer and fasting" (Mark 9:29). Prayer and fasting are the master keys to the impossible.

A fast can open up new dimensions of faith that one has never experienced before. Yet if human pride should enter into the fast, then Satan has something to work on. And that is the time in which the devil is busy. *It was after Christ's long fast that Satan came to Jesus and offered Him the kingdoms of the world.* He, however, had nothing in Christ, and his offer was indignantly refused. But the devil never gives up, and he still continues to play on human ego.

We have seen men come off a long fast with a fresh anointing upon their lives. Others have come forth with a spirit of contention quite unlike that of Christ. Some have claimed that during a fast they have received some new "revelation" that was clearly out of the mainstream of the gospel. The devil had come to them and they did not know it.

At all times there is but one place of safety for the believer and that is at the foot of the Cross. God used humble men to raise up the Pentecostal movement and has blessed it in an amazing way, so that today many in the historic churches have come to receive their share of the blessing. But Jesus gave a word of warning when He said, "The first shall be last and the last first." Let Pentecostals or anyone else become complacent or proud in the blessing that God has given them and begin to say as the Pharisees that they are not as other men, and they may suddenly discover that the blessing has departed.

Some years ago in the Spirit the Lord gave us these words of prophecy on prayer. They point out that only through the united prayer of God's people can we expect another great revival and that only through prevailing prayer will the church be brought together and made ready for the coming of the Lord!

This prophecy has been published before, but we believe it is significant to our subject, and we include it here:

> "Thou shalt begin to pray that I will assemble people and that I will bring people all agreeing together, and thou needest not worry, but thou needest to intercede and pray with divine power and divine supplications and intercessions. And the angels of God shall be camped around thee to protect thee against the violence of Satan, and the Spirit within thee shall teach thee how to pray and when to pray. For a regular hour was established in the temple of the Lord, and so it shall be established in Israel. For my people are like scattered sheep. The people of my body have not come together even yet as one people; they are not united fully. For my Spirit shall come upon them to pray day and night. For I shall have a world prayer band. And they shall pray alone and pray together, and there shall be ones and twos and threes, and there shall be thousands that pray daily
>
> "And so hath the Lord designed a great and mighty move of prayer in the very thing of intercession and rejoicings and thanksgivings. So that the intercession shall be tempered with thanksgiving . . . For were there no joy for the intercessor, then thou will be silent continuously. But the Lord will have thee to know that He will give thee rejoicings, so that it will temper the power of intercession, of weeping and mourning and crying out. And supplications shall have their courses. So intercession shall follow supplication, and there shall be thanksgivings and rejoicings and again intercessions and thanksgivings and rejoicings and petitions and requests and repenting, and all the conditions of the prophet of old will be repeated."

On still another occasion, the Lord spoke of the ministry of prayer against the powers of darkness. He said:

> "Prove me saith the Lord. Press into my presence, for the powers of darkness are against you. But I say unto you that if ye press into my presence and prove me, I will prove to you that I am God. I will prove to you that I am behind the clouds, that I am in the heaven and that I hold the world in my hand. Yea, I hold the heavens and the earth and all those things that are therein, even every man. Everyone in the earth is mine. And now the Lord thy God shall see that the harvest is completed. And there shall be a great seething. Oh my people shall pray. My people shall work. Now is the time to encourage those who by sorrows are oppressed by the circumstances

22

coming on the earth. Yea, they shall seek me early. Yea, they shall pray the Lord of the harvest. Thousands, many thousands of souls shall be rescued before the very end of the harvest comes, when they shall say the summer is ended, the harvest is past, and we are not saved."

Now may we add this word to the pastor of every church. If you have not instituted a prayer band in your church, now is the time to do so. Do not delay. Establish an hour of prayer. Get those who cannot come to the prayer services to set an hour of prayer at their homes. By so doing you are setting in motion one of the most powerful forces in the universe. This power will be working for you and your church continually. Do not restrict praying for your church alone. Pray God's kingdom to come. Pray the Lord of the harvest that He will send forth laborers into His vineyard. Pray for the Body of Christ that it may be ready at the time of His coming. Pray for the peace of Jerusalem. At all events pray, and keep the prayer band going.

CHAPTER 6

The Pentecostal Ministry

As the basis of salvation lies in the Cross, likewise the basis of the apostolic ministry lies in the baptism of the Holy Spirit which John the Baptist declared Christ would give to His followers (Matt. 3:11). The Lord in His last words before His ascension referred to this prophecy of the Baptist:

> "For John truly baptized with water; but ye shall be baptized with the Holy Ghost not many days hence" (Acts 1:5).

This was fulfilled in the mighty baptism that the 120 disciples received on the day of Pentecost:

> "And when the day of Pentecost was fully come, they were all with one accord in one place. And suddenly there came a sound from heaven as of a rushing mighty wind, and it filled all the house where they were sitting. And there appeared unto them cloven tongues like as of fire, and it sat upon each of them. And they were all filled with the Holy Ghost, and began to speak with other tongues, as the Spirit gave them utterance" (Acts 2:1-4).

Although Bible students have agreed that the experience of the disciples at Pentecost was subsequent to their salvation (Luke 10:20), it has been held by a considerable number of theologians that all believers now receive the baptism of the Spirit the moment they accept Christ. That this is not correct is evident for a number of reasons. Christ Himself in Luke 11:13 said that the Spirit was given to those who ask the Heavenly Father for it. The sinner does not ask for the Holy Spirit; he asks forgiveness for his sins. Again during Philip's revival in Samaria, many were converted and baptized in water; but they did not receive the Holy Spirit until Peter and John prayed for them, laying hands on them (Acts 8:14-17). Likewise, Paul, although he was converted on the Damascus road, did not receive the Holy Spirit baptism until three days later when Ananias prayed for him (Acts 9:17). Paul, coming to Ephesus met certain disciples and said, "Have ye received the Holy Ghost since ye believed?" indicating that he knew that the Holy Spirit did not automatically fall on a person when he first believed. Of course, every Christian has some measure of the Spirit as shown in I Corinthians 12:3 and Romans 8:9, but the *baptism in the Spirit* is something that transcends this, as Jesus declared in John 7:37-39:

> "In the last day, that great day of the feast, Jesus stood and cried, saying, If any man thirst, let him come unto me, and drink. He that believeth on me, as the scripture hath said, out of his belly shall flow rivers of living water. (But this spake he of the Spirit, which they that believe on him should receive: for the Holy Ghost was not yet given; because that Jesus was not yet glorified)."

It is not necessary to discuss at length the basis upon which the Holy Spirit is given. Certainly it is a free gift of God and is not given as the result of the candidate's achieving a certain state of holiness or perfection. The Corinthian Church was marked by immaturity and carnality; yet we observe that the gifts of the Spirit were strongly in evidence among them. Failure to understand that the Holy Spirit is given as a gift and not by merit has kept thousands of earnest people from receiving. They suppose their failure to receive is because they have not attained to a high enough degree of holiness. Yet how can one bear the fruits of the Spirit until he has received the Spirit?

There is, however, some preparation necessary before a person receives the Holy Spirit baptism. John, who foretold the coming of the Holy Spirit spoke to the people saying, "Prepare ye the way of the Lord, make his paths straight" (Luke 3:4). There is such a thing as preparing one's heart (II Chron. 19:3; 27:6). Simon the sorcerer sought to obtain the Holy Spirit and His gifts, but his heart was not right with God; and Peter, detecting his hypocrisy, rebuked him severely. Nevertheless, once a man has truly repented of his sins and turned to the Lord with all of his heart, he is ready to receive the Holy Spirit without further delay.

The baptism of the Spirit may be received directly, as it occurred on the day of Pentecost and also at the house of Cornelius. Nevertheless, the laying on of hands was the most common means in apostolic days of ministering the Spirit. This was the method used by Peter and John in Samaria. When they laid hands on the candidates, they immediately received. This was the way that Paul

25

received the Holy Spirit (Acts 9:17). It was also the method the apostles used in imparting the Holy Spirit to others at Ephesus (Acts 19:6).

Jesus in His Great Commission said that one of the signs to follow believers was that "they shall speak with new tongues" (Mark 16:17). According to the record in Acts the initial evidence of the baptism of the Holy Ghost was the speaking in other tongues. This occurred on the day of Pentecost; it happened also at Cornelius' house. The Jews knew that the Gentiles had received the Holy Spirit, "for they heard them speak with tongues, and magnify God" (Acts 10:46). The apostle Paul after receiving the Holy Spirit spoke in tongues (I Cor. 14:18). Again, when he laid hands on certain disciples at Ephesus, they spoke with tongues (Acts 19:6).

In Acts 2:4 we discern a two-fold phase of the Holy Spirit baptism. First, the power and the anointing of the Spirit as the individual receives the gift, and second, the physical evidence of the Spirit's speaking through him in other tongues.

The baptism of the Spirit is a wonderful distinctive experience, although the intensity of it is not the same with all persons. Because the anointing of the Spirit is such a blessed experience, some have disregarded the speaking in other tongues. Certainly, the latter is an essential part of the experience as Isaiah 28:11-12 indicates:

> "For with stammering lips and another tongue will he speak
> to this people. To whom he said, *This is the rest wherewith*
> *ye may cause the weary to rest; and this is the refreshing*:
> *yet they would not hear.*"

The prophecy declares that the speaking in another tongue is *the rest, the refreshing.* Certainly it is not to be ignored. In a real way the speaking in tongues is a continuous miracle that the Christian can take with him all his life.

Such in brief is the New Testament teaching on the baptism in the Holy Ghost. Now a word about the gifts. The gifts of the Spirit were first of all to be miraculous signs confirming the preaching of the Word (Mark 16:15-18). In other words they were to be a powerful means of convincing unbelievers of the genuineness of the gospel message. There was no hint that these terms of the Great Commission were to be changed in any way. The need of supernatural signs is well illustrated in Elijah's challenge on Mt. Carmel, when he asked the people the question, "How long halt ye between two opinions? if the Lord be God follow him: but if Baal, then follow him . . . the people answered him not a word"

26

(I Kings 18:21). But when the fire fell miraculously from heaven in answer to Elijah's prayer, the people fell on their faces and cried, "The Lord, he is the God; the Lord, he is the God" (Verse 39).

Do ministers need signs today to convince the unsaved? In Christ's day, there were a few hundred million heathen. Now there are nearly ten times as many! The answer is surely apparent.

The Scriptures teach that the overall purpose of the ministry-gifts is to manifest Christ's body on earth:

"Now ye are the body of Christ, and members in particular. And God hath set some in the church, first apostles, secondarily prophets, thirdly teachers, after that miracles, then gifts of healings, helps, governments, diversities of tongues" (I Cor. 12:27, 28).

The ministry-gifts function in several ways: (1) in evangelizing the world; (2) in edifying the church; (3) in bringing deliverance to God's people; (4) in perfecting the church (Eph. 4:11-13).

In the operation of the gifts of the Spirit, there are many variations, as I Corinthians 12:5-7 declares:

"And there are differences of administrations, but the same Lord. And there are diversities of operations, but it is the same God which worketh all in all. But the manifestation of the Spirit is given to every man to profit withal."

Diversities of gifts, differences of administration and diversities of operation—God is a God of variety in nature or in the spiritual realm! Every gift in its operation is in some way unique and different from that possessed by any other person.

Wonderful as these gifts are, manifestations of the Spirit may be counterfeited. We are informed by John that not every spirit is of God (I John 4:1-3). It is important, therefore, to test or try the spirits to see if they are of God or of Satan. The magicians of Moses' day were able to duplicate some of the miracles which the prophet performed, although there were definite limits to their powers (Exod. 7:9, 11-12, 19-21; 8:5-6, 18-19).

The fact that the sorcerers of Pharaoh were able to imitate these signs shows that Satan has a certain degree of power, a circumstance that we dare not ignore. Here is where some people are led astray. They suppose that everything supernatural is of God. Unfortunately, this is not true. Although we should honor the office of a prophet, there is no excuse for us to shut our eyes to the point at which we cannot recognize wrong when it exists.

"The gifts and callings of God are without repentance" (Romans

11:29).The Scriptures indicate that a gift of the Spirit may be manifested through a person (at least for a season) after he has departed from the ways of righteousness. This is something hard for some to understand; yet it was obviously portrayed in the life of Saul, who was not only king of Israel, but also had a prophet's ministry. When he became disobedient, the Spirit of the Lord departed from him for a season, and an evil spirit took its place. Yet, he was temporarily delivered, and the Spirit of God came upon him again. This conflict between good and evil continued in Saul's life until at length, because of continued disobedience, the evil powers finally predominated. One should study the following Scriptures carefully which relate to Saul's decline: I Samuel 10:6, 10; 16:14-16, 23; 18:10; 19:23-24; 28:6-7.

Important as the gifts of the Spirit are, they must be accompanied by the fruits. This Paul brings out clearly in I Corinthians 13:1-3:

> "Though I speak with the tongues of men and angels, and have not charity, I am become as sounding brass or a tinkling cymbal. And though I have the gift of prophecy, and understand all mysteries, and all knowledge; and though I have all faith, so that I could remove mountains, and have not charity, I am nothing."

Miracles, martyrdom, generous giving to the poor all profit nothing unless divine love and compassion are the motives behind them.

There is a definite need for ministers who have a special ministry of the Holy Spirit. Philip had a powerful revival in Samaria, but none received the Holy Spirit until Peter and John came down and laid their hands on them. Then many were filled with the Holy Spirit. God has used individuals, who though they did not have an evangelistic ministry, have brought many into the experience of the baptism of the Holy Spirit.

28

CHAPTER 7

What Every Minister Should Know About the Gift of Prophecy

These are the days when prophetic gifts are attracting a great deal of attention. Psychics are setting themselves up as having the genuine gift of prophecy, although their predictions on the whole are little more than fortune telling. It is clear that Satan's emissaries are hard at work in this field. *Yet there are true prophetic gifts, and the genuine should not be shunned because counterfeits exist.* It is important, therefore, that a minister be sufficiently acquainted with the gift that he can distinguish between the true and the false, and thus be able to guide his people along Scriptural lines.

In the Old Testament the prophetic ministry was essentially *foretelling.* In the New Testament, the emphasis is on *forthtelling.* In other words, as the apostle declares "he that prophesieth speaketh unto men to edification, and exhortation, and comfort" (I Cor. 14:3). When man was placed in the Garden of Eden, God conversed with him directly. That communion was broken by man's disobedience. In a certain sense, the gift of prophecy restores that direct communion.

The prophetic gift has many variations. It may be exhortational; it may take the form of song or poetry as in the Psalms; or it may on occasion reveal future events. The gift has varied operations and in some instances may be a vehicle for other gifts such as the word of wisdom, the word of knowledge, or discerning of spirits.

Prophecy relating to the future is of two distinct kinds. Some prophecies are unconditional as for example, the Abrahamic covenant or the Messianic prophecies. Others are conditional such as Isaiah's warning of Hezekiah's impending death (II Kings 20:1-6) or Jonah's pronouncement of judgment on Nineveh (Jonah 3:3-10). Unconditional prophecies are not dependent upon man for fulfillment. *Conditional prophecies, however, depend on the obedience of the person or persons to whom they are addressed.*

There is a difference between revelation prophecy and that which

29

is exhortational. In the latter, the Spirit of God takes over the person's subconscious mind and from his storehouse selects, rearranges, and anoints certain truths for the edification of the hearers. Revelation prophecy is a higher form of the gift and involves a greater yielding to the Spirit. Exhortational prophecy is the more prevalent and usually is the kind manifested in regular services (I Cor. 14:26).

It is true that there is an increasing hunger in the hearts of the people for revelation prophecy. Nevertheless, because of the complexity of the gift, certain safeguards are important in its operation. The gift of prophecy involves the merging of the human and the divine, the finite with the infinite, the imperfect with the perfect. This is something most people, even some ministers do not understand. If prophecy were entirely an operation of God, there would be no need of instruction in its exercise. *God does not need instruction.*

The inspiration and revelation gifts are, therefore, a product of both God and man. God is infallible, and when the person is fully yielded to the Spirit, the utterances are infallible. Unfortunately, a man is not always fully yielded. Therefore, Paul tells us that prophecies are to be judged to make certain that they fully conform to the Word (I Cor. 14:29).

"The testimony of Jesus is the spirit of prophecy" (Rev. 19:10). True prophecy ever points to Christ, to His deity, His ministry, His purpose in coming into the world, and to His return to earth. Alleged prophetic gifts that engage in telling fortunes, divining mysteries, predicting the outcome of political events, locating lost articles, etc., betray the fact that they are something other than the Bible gift. The true gift of prophecy is not to be confused with fortune-telling, extra-sensory perception, clairvoyance, and other psychic manifestations. It may, however, at times give guidance and counsel. It is important, nonetheless, that people should search the Scriptures first before looking for further guidance. Moreover, just as some people misinterpret Scripture, so it is possible to misinterpret a prophecy. In all cases people need spiritual discernment to understand either.

Old Testament prophets on occasion failed to recognize the time of fulfillment of their prophecies. Some make that mistake today. For example the Bible speaks of apocalyptic judgments taking place during the Great and Terrible Day of the Lord. That time is not far off, but it has not yet come. When folk are given the impression that some catastrophic event is to happen immediately, and it fails to take place, they are prone to lose confidence in the gift altogether.

For example, a few years ago a man prophesied that Dallas would be destroyed within seven days. He took his predictions to the newspapers and said that he was speaking for a Christian business group. We warned the leaders of the local chapter to repudiate any association with this individual and his prophecies, as it was evident that he was under the influence of seducing spirits. This they did, and well it was that they did; for the seven days came and went, and nothing happened.

It is true that God does give certain kinds of guidance by means of the revelation gifts. Such was the warning received by Paul when he was on his way to Jerusalem (Acts 20:22-23). Even so, the prophecy had to be correctly interpreted. But Paul interpreted the prophecy only as a warning of what would happen to him if he went to Jerusalem; he did not see it as a prohibition. The apostle went on to his destination, apparently in the will of God, although it happened to him, even as the prophecy said.

The gift is not intended as a vehicle to establish new doctrine. We are warned by Peter of men who will come into the church with "damnable heresies" which can lead to great confusion. Some of the most serious heresies owe their origin to the "private interpretation" of some self-styled prophet.

One woman highly acclaimed today as a prophetess claims to get her prophecies from a serpent. Although she professes to be a religious woman, she apparently does not realize that the serpent is a symbol of Satan. This reveals the true source of her prophecies.

Despite these cautions, let us say that we sorely need the inspiration and revelation gifts in operation in the church. May God give His ministers discernment to distinguish between the true and the false. Paul commands us to "despise not prophesyings. Prove all things; hold fast that which is good" (I Thes. 5:20-21).

The other gift which has a prominent place in public ministry is the gift of healing. It is very important that every minister should have some knowledge of how the healing ministry operates. We shall consider this subject in the following chapter.

CHAPTER 8

Important Facts About the Healing Ministry

The potential of the healing ministry to reach the masses has been abundantly demonstrated. No apologies need be made for it, although for it to function effectively, great wisdom is required. The ministry of Christ was essentially one of healing for both soul and body. The Lord, quoting from the prophecy of Isaiah, declared this in His sermon which He delivered in the city Nazareth:

> "The Spirit of the Lord is upon me, because he hath anointed me to preach the gospel to the poor; he hath sent me to heal the broken-hearted, to preach deliverance to the captives, and recovering of sight to the blind, to set at liberty them that are bruised, To preach the acceptable year of the Lord" (Luke 4:18-19).

This healing ministry of Christ and His disciples was no improvisation, but was in full harmony with the church's mission to the world. When the Lord called His disciples, He commissioned them to preach saying, "The kingdom of heaven is at hand. Heal the sick, cleanse the lepers, raise the dead, cast out devils: freely ye have received, freely give" (Matt. 10:7-8). He gave the same commission to seventy other disciples and then to all believers (Luke 10:9).

The Lord showed the potential of the ministry by declaring that if Sodom and Gomorrah had witnessed the mighty miracles that He had performed in the cities about the Sea of Galilee, they would have repented (Matt. 11:23). In His Great Commission to the church He said among other things, "And these signs shall follow them that believe . . . they shall lay hands on the sick, and they shall recover" (Mark 16:17-18).

Evangelization by signs, wonders, and miracles was the method used in the days of the apostles. The disciples of Jesus understood what was required of them when they prayed, "Grant unto thy servants, that with all boldness they may speak thy word, By

32

stretching forth thine hand to heal; and that signs and wonders may be done by the name of the holy child Jesus (Acts 4:29, 30; Acts 4-5). It was a visitation in which the gifts of healing were powerfully in evidence; even mass healings were indicated (Acts 5:15, 16). Although there arose fierce opposition by the unbelieving clergy (Acts 5:17), God's ministers refused to give heed to the threatenings of men, and they continued their fearless preaching (Acts 5:21).

The healing ministry is the gospel in action. Through it multitudes have been awakened and brought to the realization that Christ is the Saviour. In recent years the salvation-healing revivals have attracted world-wide attention. Audiences have numbered up to 200,000 people, with large numbers accepting Christ. These are documented facts.

One of the oddest arguments against the healing ministry has been the statement that it is more important to preach salvation than healing. The irony of this is that the healing ministry has often provided far more candidates for salvation than available workers were able to take care of. The truth is that the two ministries are complementary. To neglect one is to cause the other to suffer. Christ, the great winner of souls, did not consider that His healing of the sick hindered Him in reaching the lost. Just the opposite was true. When Jesus sent His disciples to preach the gospel, He said, "Preach the kingdom of God, and heal the sick" (Luke 9:2). According to the New Testament, Christ spent about three fourths of his time healing the sick.

The assumption that divine healing is something unspiritual is a strange error. The Pharisees contended that Jesus should not heal on the Sabbath day because in their opinion healing was something to be done only on work days. Jesus repudiated this idea by healing on the Sabbath.

Why do some oppose healing? There are different reasons. The Sadducees who were the modernists of that day, committed themselves to a rationalism that denied the supernatural. As for the Pharisees the case was different. They were fundamentalists, and the reason they opposed Christ's healing ministry was because of the popular reception given to it and their own inability to duplicate it.

They reasoned among themselves saying, "What do we? for this man doeth many miracles. If we let him alone, all men will believe on him" (John 11:47-48). The truth was that the Pharisees were willing to believe in the miracles of the past but wanted none at present. Their attitude led them on dangerous ground of actually claiming that the healing was the work of the devil. The Lord solemnly warned them that they were guilty of blaspheming and were in fact in danger of committing the unpardonable sin (Matt. 12:31-32).

The ministry of healing is one requiring a strong faith and special wisdom on the part of the minister. The novice can make serious mistakes. For one thing, teaching should always precede the ministering to the sick if the best results are to be realized.

Healing is for all even as salvation is for all; but all who come for healing are not healed, any more than all who come for salvation are saved. There are conditions attached to both. Much depends on the kind of instruction that is given to the candidates. "Faith cometh by hearing and hearing by the word of God." In Nazareth, Christ could do no mighty miracles, because of the unbelief of the people (Mark 6:5). They would not listen to His instructions and in fact tried to take His life. It is not surprising that few were healed in that place. At Bethesda Jesus saw a multitude of impotent folk, yet He healed one and departed. The conditions evidently were not right. To the one He did heal He said, "Behold, thou art made whole: sin no more, lest a worse thing come unto thee" (John 5:14).

The time required for a healing depends on the measure of faith present both in the one who ministers and the one who receives. Not all healings are instantaneous. Jesus said to the nobleman, "Except ye see signs and wonders, ye will not believe" (John 4:48). The nobleman accepted the admonition and went his way believing, and his son "began to amend from that hour" (Verse 52).

The blind man of Bethsaida did not receive perfect sight when Christ first ministered to him (Mark 8:24). The ten lepers were cleansed only as they went. Faith is an act (Luke 17:14). Christ's promise to believers that "they shall lay hands on the sick; and they shall recover:" implies gradual healing rather than an instantaneous miracle. Of course in the healing meetings there are miracles that take place instantaneously. But there will be others who are healed that will receive strength gradually.

The minister must instruct the people after receiving deliverance, even more than before. Jesus gave a warning that an affliction may come back upon a man who puts forth no effort to arm himself against the counterattacks of the enemy (Luke 11:24-26). Some have supposed that when a genuine miracle takes place, it is impossible for the recipient to lose it. That is not Scriptural. Peter walked on the water which was a miracle. *But when he took his eyes off Christ and looked upon circumstances and conditions, he began to sink.* So those who get their eyes off the Lord and His promises and look at symptoms may well have a recurrence of their affliction.

The Scriptures clearly teach there are hindrances that can keep a person from receiving healing. For example, failure to take proper care of one's body can result in serious illness. Epaphroditus, due to overwork and strain almost died from what appears to have been nervous exhaustion; nevertheless, through Paul's prayers, he recovered (Phil. 2:25-30).

Perhaps the most common omission in the .divine healing ministry is that preachers do not instruct folk after they get healed to move on up into the realm of divine health. *Health should be the normal experience of every Christian.* This was God's plan for the believers even in the Old Testament days (Exod. 15:25-26; 23:25). It is God's plan for the believer today (III John 2). Those who seek repeated healings often find it is increasingly hard to get deliverance. Some folk make it a habit to ask for prayer every time there is a prayer line. People should be taught that divine health is God's plan for them. Sickness should be the exception. Every Christian should read the 91st Psalm over and over until it becomes a part of him.

Disease is definitely associated with Satan as the Scriptures clearly state (Job 2:7; Acts 10:38). But many afflictions are indirectly caused by Satan and are more accurately described as oppression. That is something different from demon possession. No evil spirit can possess the soul of the believer, although if he fails to claim his rights, Satan may oppress his body. There are many cases in which Christians are oppressed by the enemy, and they need to be loosed from that bondage. This is clearly shown in the instance in which Christ liberated a daughter of Abraham bound by Satan for 18 years (Luke 13:16). She was a daughter of promise, but Satan had her bound.

Because God gives a man an outstanding ministry of healing does not necessarily guarantee that his conduct is always pleasing to God. Judas evidently had a healing ministry. Acts 1:17 says that he "obtained part of this ministry." But that he sadly failed no one denies. The fall of Judas, however, in no way invalidated the ministry of healing. To condemn healing because someone who practices it fails, is mischievous. Some ministers who preach salva-

35

tion fail. Should we, therefore, condemn salvation? Divine healing is a reality because God's Word says it is. A thousand miracles cannot make the promise stronger; a thousand failures cannot make it weaker.

Occasionally an opposer of healing will challenge a minister to perform a miracle to prove that healing is genuine. While God often allows miracles to occur that have convinced infidels and skeptics, we do not find Christ accepting challenges. He never tried to prove He was a wonder-worker. Jesus rejected Satan's challenge to perform a miracle by making bread out of stones, although later He provided bread for 5,000. He refused to cast Himself down from the temple when the devil suggested that by doing so He could prove that He was the Son of God. Later He overruled the power of gravity when He walked on the water to meet His disciples who were in jeopardy on the sea. When the Pharisees clamored for a "sign from heaven," the Lord refused to grant them one (Matt. 16:1-3).

Christ's healing ministry was based on compassion for the sick and those out of the way rather than the providing of wonders for skeptics and those who opposed Him. To the helpless and needy, He ministered His healing power freely. He did not perform His miracles in a corner where no one could see them, although He never went out of His way to convince skeptics.

Demonstration of miracles before the audience does have an important purpose. Christ performed them in full view of the multitudes. In working with various evangelists we have often been able to help them by showing them the most effective way to minister to the sick in public services. It is a common problem that chronic seekers who have little faith will rush forward to get to the head of the prayer line. Their lack of faith may hinder those who follow. The evangelist should feel free to minister to those who he sees have faith first. The apostle Paul followed this method (Acts 14:9, 10). Building faith in the audience makes it possible for greater miracles to occur.

When faith reaches a certain point, it may be possible to pray a mass prayer in which many are healed at one time.

At all healing services, ample opportunity should be given for sinners to accept Christ. In such meetings we have seen many hundreds respond to a single invitation.

Inquirers after being instructed should be sent to a special prayer room. In foreign lands it is not unusual for thousands of people to respond to a single altar call. In such cases special convert classes should be conducted for the seekers, preferably on the following morning. If possible, appropriate literature and New Testaments should be made available to the newly converted.

Much more could be written on the subject. But enough has been said to show that the healing ministry is solidly based on Bible grounds and is a most valuable means of evangelizing the multitudes.

Of course, after the campaign is over, special measures should be taken to establish the converts firmly in the faith.

While this chapter has been devoted chiefly to divine healing as an instrument of mass evangelism, it can also be a powerful means in the hands of the pastor to evangelize his community. This has been proven again and again. The afflicted are ever with us. When the news gets around that the sick are being healed, new people will be coming to the services. It is indeed significant that many pastors in the historic churches are now conducting regular healing services with reports of outstanding results.

CHAPTER 9

The Magic Power of Faith

Of course there is nothing really magic about faith, except that the results of it are so remarkable that it appears to the uninitiated as magic. Faith is the power that brought the worlds into existence. Faith is the power that changes the impossible to the possible. Faith turns defeat into victory, sickness into health, darkness into light. Faith turns a dream into reality. Now God has given a measure of His faith to every born-again man, and all may use it if they will.

Indeed, even the nominal Christians are exercising human faith in the natural and psychic spheres. Jesus once said: "The children of this world are in their generation wiser than the children of light" (Luke 16:8). Not wiser in eternity, of course, but wiser for the time in which they live. His words have a strange application today in the cults that invoke the laws of faith which properly belong only to the children of God! They have brashly moved into the faith realm, using that power in the lower spheres for material benefits, without reference to spiritual things. For faith produces results in those lower realms as well as the spiritual sphere. That is the reason that the magicians of Pharaoh could duplicate some of the miracles of Moses, although there were definite limits beyond which they could not go (Exod. 7:9-21; 8:5-19).

These metaphysical cults operate under various names such as Unity, Truth, New Thought, Rosicrucianism, Coueism, etc. . . . Although they do not accept the blood atonement, their practicioners, by taking advantage of the powers of the mind, are able to accomplish certain mental and physical cures. Through the powers of suggestion, they profess to bring new hope, health, happiness, financial success, personal security to their devotees. This is a doctrine of materialism, but it has an appeal to the natural mind and is attracting an ever-increasing following.

Yet the Lord has offered His followers all that these cults can offer and a thousand times more. Jesus Christ not only has promised life more abundantly in this time, but in the world to come, life everlasting. Satan suffers his greatest blow when a soul accepts Christ as his Saviour. He, therefore, is determined if possible to keep that person from obtaining his rights as a believer. While Satan permits the false cults to teach their followers that they can all have an abundance of material things—health, happiness, and prosperity—he seeks if possible to delude Christians into believing that God makes them sick, that they must suffer disease for His glory, and they must struggle through life in grinding poverty. We strongly protest the idea that sickness, poverty, and failure should be the lot of the Christian.

Christ has given to His people the use of His Name by which they can appropriate all that they need. There is indeed a heavenly magic in that Name! The minister who sets a faith course, who assumes a life-attitude of believing, will find that things will continually work out in his favor instead of against him. Joseph in comforting his repentant brethren over their past misdeeds said, "But as for you, ye thought evil against me, but God meant it unto good" (Gen. 50:20). We are not speaking of faith operating in the psychological realm; we are referring to the faith that operates in the spiritual realm. There is an important distinction to be made. Some have said that it does not matter what you believe, just so you believe. This is as false as can be. True faith is faith in God's promises. It is faith in the Name of Jesus. "What things soever ye desire, when you pray, believe ye receive them, and ye shall have them" (Mark 11:24).

In some of the chapters, we deal with problems of the minister. While I was writing along that line, the Spirit of the Lord spoke to me and said, "Be careful in your instructions that you do not become negative, but keep always on the faith line." How imporant that is! When we see the mistakes of some preachers and how they have damaged their ministries, our attention may be focused too strongly on men's mistakes instead of God's Word. To avoid mistakes is important, but that alone is not sufficient to bring success. Those in the cemetery make no mistakes, but neither do they accomplish anything! The minister must move out into the faith realm if he is to reach his goal.

Man was created to rule. He was made in the image of God and given dominion over the earth. If he fears God he need fear nothing else. Man lost all by the Fall; yet through Christ he recovers all and more. As a minister of the gospel, the man of God has been given authority to loose those who are in prison and to bring deliverance to those who are bound.

One of the most common faults of some preachers is that they tend to be too negative. A minister may bear down on sin, but he must also balance his message with faith that will lift the people up out of their sin and weakness. A heavy sermon without the element of faith in it can leave the people oppressed rather than lifted. The minister must bear in mind that "the letter killeth but the Spirit maketh alive." Many church members already know that they are living a defeated life. The minister must break the yoke; he must inspire them to move up into a realm of faith where victory is. They will not find it by looking inwardly at themselves. If their attention is focused on their faults, they will remain in the same condition. They must turn away from themselves to the promise, to Christ and to His power to deliver.

The preacher, before he can minister effectively to others, must first partake of the fruits. He must practice what he preaches. It is disturbing indeed to hear someone say, "I pray for others and they are healed, but I cannot get healing myself." A successful preacher must be victorious in all departments of his life—body, soul, and spirit. God intends that His ministers shall be full overcomers in every sense of the word.

Apostolic ministry, therefore, is basically a faith ministry. It is not to be confused with the psychic operations of the mental cults. This power comes not from the mind, but from another source—the Lord Jesus Christ. Through the use of His Name, He has given us power that transcends and goes beyond all other powers.

> "And whatsoever ye shall ask in my name, that will I do, that the Father may be glorified in the Son. If ye shall ask any thing in my name, I will do it" (John 14:13-14).
>
> "Ye have not chosen me, but I have chosen you, and ordained you, that ye should go and bring forth fruit, and that your fruit should remain: that whatsoever ye shall ask of the Father in my name, he may give it you" (John 15:16).

What tremendous power is represented in that Name! The apostles used it with an abandonment, and it should be so used today. What does it mean to use the Name? It means that we have power of attorney; we have the authority to use all the might back of that Name. All that Christ could do when He was on earth can now be done by the believer who uses His Name in faith. This is the reason that Christ said the believer would do the works that He did and even greater works (John 14:12).

At times the church has gotten a brief glimpse of the potential power of the Name and has experienced the authority invested in it.

The blind have been made to see, the deaf to hear, and the lame to walk. Even death has given way before that Name. Praying in the Name of Jesus means the believer is acting as the representative of the absent Christ and is using His authority to fulfill His will on earth. Through it, he has power to deliver humanity that is bound and in the toils of Satan.

The minister will find that there is a class of people who are always trying but who never succeed in obtaining what they want. They are ever asking for prayers but do not succeed in getting any further. Many are held by habits such as tobacco, liquor, or lusts. They are in fact bound by an unseen power. What they need is someone to break that power in the Name of Jesus. Through the power of that Name, they can be delivered instantaneously.

The young minister, therefore, must not settle for less than a supernatural ministry. He must reach out and claim this power that will set people free. How can that power be applied? The answer is simple. It is appropriated by faith. Jesus gave us the great faith promise in Mark 11:22-24:

> "And Jesus answering saith unto them, Have faith in God. For verily I say unto you, That whosoever shall say unto this mountain, Be thou removed, and be thou cast into the sea; and shall not doubt in his heart, but shall believe that those things which he saith shall come to pass; he shall have whatsoever he saith. Therefore I say unto you, What things soever ye desire, when ye pray, believe that ye receive them, and ye shall have them."

Here revealed is the secret of faith, the means by which the power behind the Name can be released. *Faith does not look at circumstances nor conditions, but at the promise.* Christ spoke these words in connection with the cursing of the fig tree. At the instant He spoke the words, nothing appeared to happen. The disciples looked at the tree, and the leaves seemed as healthy as ever. But they saw only with their natural sight. They were merely believing what they saw, and that is why many people's faith doesn't work. They look at circumstances, at the conditions, at their symptoms, and at their feelings. They believe only what their natural eye sees. *But a man of God must look past these things at the Word, at the promise.* He must believe he receives. Later he will see with the natural eye. Jesus did not look at the leaves of the tree after He cursed it. By the eye of faith He saw the roots dry up.

We must remember that faith is only faith when we don't feel anything nor see anything. That is the only time we can exercise

41

faith. Faith is something apart from what we see. Doubts begin when we base belief upon what we see rather than upon God's promise. Faith is not some mysterious thing—working up a strange feeling. *It is the irrevocable decision of the soul to base its belief upon what God has said.*

Jesus said, "What things soever ye desire, when ye pray, believe that ye receive them, and ye shall have them." In other words we are to consider the miracle as already having taken place. The minister is to reckon the answer to prayer as already in his hand. He is to visualize the answer. *That is the secret: visualize the answer.*

Jesus said that the believer shall have "whatsoever he saith." This is important. One rises no higher than his confession. Some pray for deliverance, but after they get through, instead of proclaiming deliverance they confess weakness, sickness, and doubt. Jesus said we shall get what we say. Say the wrong thing, and the law will work against you. You still get what you say, but it is the wrong thing.

Ministers, as well as those in the pew, are not immune from this error. Some confess failure, and they have failure. We have seen some of the most spiritual people insist that they are still sick after they have been prayed for a hundred times. They have gotten what they confessed. They cry for a miracle, but they reject God's way of getting that miracle. His Word says, "Believe ye receive and ye shall have." They say, "Not so, Lord. I will believe after I feel well and strong and not before." And so they never get deliverance.

How well I remember the time when I was really tested to the point of death. It appeared that prayer had failed to change or to check the course of a carbuncle that had spread from ear to ear. With all strength gone, I could pray no more. When it seemed that life itself was slipping away, I made a decision. I said, "Lord it looks as if all hope is gone, but whatever happens, just for your record, I say that I am healed; I shall get well." What happened? Four days later I was back in the house of God. Hezekiah was healed of a carbuncle and went up to the house of God on the third day (II Kings 20:1-11). He bettered my record by one day! I said I was healed when everything seemed against me. I got what I said.

A minister must first be a partaker of the fruits. If he believes in divine healing, he ought to claim that promise for his household. He should stand on God's Word which declares that He "shall bless thy bread, and thy water; and I will take sickness away from the midst of thee" (Exod. 23:25). True, Satan will contest every new step of faith, but the fruits of the victory are sweet and worth the cost a hundred times over.

God intends that His ministers shall be financially solvent. As John says, "Beloved I wish above all things that thou mayest prosper and be in health even as thy soul prospereth" (III John 2). What a pity to see a minister slinking away from his creditors. He has lost his dignity as a minister. As a child of God, let him claim the promise. Jesus said, "Verily, verily, I say unto you, Whatsoever ye shall ask the Father in my name, he will give it to you" (John 16:23-24). God will supply a minister's material needs without his having to resort to methods that are suspect. God gives victory in this area as well as in any other.

And how shall it be with his family? Preachers as well as others experience trials in raising a family. Their children pass through vicissitudes and moods the same as others. But a minister can believe for his sons and daughters so that in time they will surely come out victorious. By faith the man of God can commit them into the hands of God and say to Satan as Moses said to Pharaoh, "Not a hoof shall be left behind."

The minister must be on the alert that nowhere does Satan make a breakthrough. A general in battle watches to see that his ranks are unbroken. For if the enemy cannot break through at one point, he will attack from the rear. A Christian carries his shield of faith in front; therefore, he must keep his line of defense intact at all points. By using this shield, he can withstand all the fiery darts of the enemy.

Christ said, "All power in heaven and earth is delivered unto me". In turn He delegates this power to us through the use of His Name. Let us as ministers of the living God appropriate that power and go forth to liberate humanity from its sin and sickness.

In the chapters which follow, we deal with some of the problems of ministers. Many of these problems are created because the minister has moved out of the faith realm, or has in some way departed from the known will of God. This departure can surely affect the operation of faith. Jesus said, "If ye abide in me and my words abide in you, ye shall ask what ye will and it shall be done unto you." To live in the realm of faith means we must day by day stay close to God. As we abide in His presence and maintain an unswerving attitude of faith, we shall find things working together for us rather than against us.

CHAPTER 10

Why Some Ministers Fail

And now we come to the subject of why some ministers fail. It certainly is unfortunate that anyone called of God should fail. The purpose of these pages is to call attention to those peculiar snares of the enemy who is ever probing to find a weak point in a minister's armor. How sad it is to see a man's ministry develop to a certain point and then lose its momentum and begin to decline. Certainly this should not be. As a minister gains more experience he should become more proficient. His faith should rise to higher heights. He should be achieving greater victories. The high-water mark of a man's ministry should not be reached until the hour arrives for God to call him home. It should be with him as it was with the prophet Daniel. Kings came and went; kingdoms rose and fell, but Daniel's fruitful ministry covered a period of almost a century. During that time he dominated the scene. His prayers resulted in his people's being restored to Jerusalem. He was given a vision of the coming of the Messiah "who would take away the sin of the world." Again He saw Him coming in glory to set up His everlasting kingdom. The life of Daniel is an excellent example for the man of God. There was no diminution of his powers throughout his life.

In the following pages we note some of the causes of why ministers fail. It is our hope that these suggestions will help preachers to be alerted to certain pitfalls and dangers and thus to avoid them.

CARELESSNESS IN MORALS

One of the most enigmatical characters in the Bible is Samson. His work and ministry was announced by an angel before he was born. He was forbidden to use strong drink; and as a Nazarite he was enjoined to lead a separated life. When he reached manhood, the Spirit of God moved upon him, and he was able to perform astounding feats requiring great physical strength. Samson possessed an unusual imagination and singlehandedly won a succession of dramatic victories over the Philistines. Being a confirmed individualist, however, the prophet always preferred to work alone.

Since he consulted no one, he lacked the stabilizing influences which come by taking counsel with others. There was no one to caution him against the weaknesses peculiar to his nature.

There were indeed serious flaws in Samson's character. He was not only headstrong, but he lacked moral perspective. While a young man, he took a wife from among the Philistines. He was like some foolish young ministers today who choose a helpmate on the basis of physical attraction without consideration of spiritual qualities. In Samson's case the episode ended in a fiasco, and ultimately in the tragic death of the young woman.

There appears to be a long gap in the Scriptural record of Samson's life. When the narrative is resumed, we find the prophet's character has sadly deteriorated. Indeed we see him actually consorting with lewd Philistine women. The puzzling circumstance is that Samson was able to go on in his role of a prophet, even after he committed these immoral acts! This may have surprised Samson himself. And here is where some people are sadly deceived. Because God does not immediately render judgment on them or remove His Spirit from them, they get a wrong impression of God's attitude toward sin. Those who commit an immoral act may at first be conscience-stricken and overwhelmed by the realization that they have broken God's moral law. But then like David they find that God has not altogether forsaken them. Some may tearfully accept God's forgiveness and firmly resolve from then on that there will never be a repetition of their indiscretion. But others instead of being appreciative and grateful for God's mercy may consider His forebearance an indication that He condones what they have done. Such persons are indeed on dangerous ground. They are in fact heading straight for disaster.

There are those who after they have committed an act of immorality begin to rationalize their deed. When the first pangs of remorse are over, they may begin to feel that what they have done is not so bad. Such a state of mind often results in another moral lapse. It is the old story of a man's adjusting his conscience to his conduct. Thus they deceive themselves into believing that God overlooks their act. Some have continued to preach while carrying on a clandestine affair with a member of their church.

But sooner or later those involved are due for a rude awakening. The words of the Scripture, "Be sure your sin will find you out," are not in vain. They have never been annulled. Some have awakened to their danger and have deeply repented, while others go on until the whole miserable story comes out in the open.

God in His mercy will forgive all sins except one. So He forgives even adultery when those who have committed it turn from it in real repentance. But often there is much heartache, loss of reputation, sometimes even a breakup of the home. God forgave David, but think how much he had to pay. He lost his children's confidence; one son betrayed him, and another sought to usurp the throne. As the prophet declared, "The sword never departed from his door."

So it was with Samson who played with fire. He lost his strength and fell into the hands of the enemy. While in captivity his eyes were put out, and he was assigned to grinding in the prison-house. Although God gave him one last opportunity to fulfill his ministry, Samson's end was sad. He wrought no abiding work in Israel.

NEGATIVE PREACHING

Ministers must take a stand against sin, and any preacher who does not do this is not true to his calling. However, with the negative there must also be the positive. And this is where many ministers fail. Their preaching lies too largely in the negative. A surgeon who probes the body for a diseased organ must not fail to bind up the wound that is made.

Some ministers mark themselves as purely preachers of the law. They are ever denouncing evil in their congregation, but they do not lift up Christ as the answer. They fail to build faith in their people or inspire them to victory. Severity in the pulpit may be necessary, but it must be constructive criticism. A preacher, therefore, who centers his preaching on the faults of his people and does not show them the way out has gone down a dead-end street. He has failed to lead them on to victory and deliverance.

A minister, therefore, must be a man with a positive message. He must create faith in his hearers. It is his duty to lift them into new dimensions of spiritual experience. He is there to point them to the prize of the mark of the high calling in Christ Jesus.

The pastor must teach his people to commit their lives into the hands of God. As the psalmist said, "Commit thy way unto the Lord; trust also in him; and he shall bring it to pass" (Psalm 37:5). He should teach them to commit their bodies into the hands of the Lord, and to do likewise with their families. He should also instruct them to commit their material needs to Him.

Here is where many ministers fail. Instead of bringing their people to a place of rest in the Lord, they wield the law as a whip, which has no power to give spiritual life.

The ministry of deliverance is set forth by Christ in Luke 4:18. The man of God as an ambassador of Christ should come armed with dominion and authority to set men free and to bring them into a place of victory in Christ. He who does this cannot fail.

A MARRIAGE OUT OF THE WILL OF GOD

Nothing can either help or hinder a minister more than his marriage, depending on whether or not he has married in the will of God. Many a man must attribute a large share of the credit for his success to a wife who has been a real helpmate to him.

Yet the number of cases in which an ill-matched marriage has ruined or seriously impaired a man's ministry is large enough to be considered a major hazard. Whatever the reasons are for which a minister enters into an ill-starred union, we can say that usually the deciding factor is that he did not pray sufficiently about it. Statistics show that young people are notoriously inept in the matter of making a correct choice of a life's partner. The number of divorces being turned out by our courts bear out only too well this sad fact. Many Christian young people cannot distinguish between a match that would have the blessing of heaven upon it and what is a mere infatuation. Human judgment is often a poor guarantee that a marriage will turn out well. If only the parties concerned would make it a matter of earnest prayer, providence would so overrule as to bring about God's will in the matter.

The ministry involves so wide a range of responsibilities and sacrifices that the woman who has not had as definite a call as her husband is apt to break under the strain. Like Job's wife, she may actually exert her influence to get him to give up the ministry. Who hasn't been witness to a case in which a man's ministry has been seriously inpaired because the wife lost interest in that kind of life or showed an inclination to worldliness?

There are women who would otherwise make good wives, but who never have experienced a real call to service. They would not dream of hindering their husbands, but they sit in the congregation and do not enter into the church's activities except in a most casual way. This is indeed unfortunate, since it sets a poor example to the rest of the women in the congregation.

On the other hand, a minister should not marry a woman solely on the basis of her abilities, since there must first of all be a real love for each other.

A marriage not based on love is in grave danger. What a minister needs is a wife who first of all will be a companion to him, then share in his problems and be able to discuss them with him intelligently. She should not just sit on the sidelines, but be able to participate in her husband's ministry in some tangible way.

The demands of the ministry actually accentuate the normal problems that are involved in marriage. When these problems are not solved and adjustments made, the situation may terminate in a separation or a divorce. Even in extreme cases in which the minister believes he has Scriptural grounds for divorce, he will—at least for a long time—labor under a severe handicap. Congregations are not eager to have a pastor serve them who is not able to solve his own problems or is even slightly involved in scandal. The result is that the man may be forced to turn to secular employment, if he does not leave the ministry altogether.

FAILURE TO REACH THE YOUTH

Some ministers pass all the tests and appear to be excellent shepherds in all respects except one. This one serious lack largely cancels out all their other successes. We refer to the inability of some ministers to understand and make rapport with youth. A pastor has a marvelous opportunity to reach young people during their impressionable years before they are committed to a life away from the church. They are there to be won for the asking. Yet it is a sad fact that in many churches there is a dearth of young people. One by one as they reach their teens, they slip away.

Youth are the life-blood to any church. The older people will gradually die off, and if there are no young people to fill the gap, the church must slowly die. The only hope for such a church is that new members will move into the neighborhood, the fruit of someone else's labors.

Some ministers can feed the older members of the flock in an acceptable way. This is important, but it is not enough. The pastor must also make provision for the younger ones. He must put forth an intelligent effort to learn how to reach them. He must remember that Christ not only told Peter to feed His sheep, but He also said, "Feed my lambs."

Youth should be won before life's patterns are set. To win them requires prevailing prayer, an imagination, and a plan to reach them. First of all, it is necessary to provide young people with legitimate activities. A choir and an orchestra come to mind as an excellent way to get many of them active in the church. However,

48

before that, there must be an effort to bring them to a decision for Christ. Adolescents are the easiest converts to make, and the easiest to hold—if a real effort is made and they are not taken for granted.

The matter of making a young people's meeting interesting is of supreme importance. It must involve more than a few songs and testimonies. There is no end to the variation of themes that can be arranged in these meetings—programs that will fascinate and hold the attention of youth. Much prayer combined with intelligent effort must play their part in the planning. There is no space here to describe or even enumerate some of the methods that can be used. If a minister does not know how to develop a vital youth program, he should study the methods of those who have been successful. Needless to say all programs must be kept spiritual and Christ-centered.

Each young person should be encouraged to receive the baptism in the Spirit. This experience will greatly deepen his spiritual outlook on life.

No minister can say he is successful who does not succeed in retaining a substantial number of the children who grow up in his church. If he is failing there, it is high time that he take inventory. Otherwise the church has nothing to look forward to but a gradual diminution resulting from the older members' dying off with no young ones to take their place.

It requires real effort to reach the young, but it can be done; and no pastor can say he is a success who fails at this crucial point.

FAILURE TO BE "DILIGENT IN BUSINESS"

A true Christian is not of this world; nevertheless, he is in this world. Therefore, the Scriptures instruct us to be subject to the powers that be. In order to obey this Scriptural admonition, we must be aware of the common laws of our land. Strange as it may seem, there are some men who are so absorbed in spiritual things that they fail to be aware of the most elementary matters of the business world.

We have known good men to disregard the income tax laws. Although their incomes were substantial they neglected to file reports. Some have actually been naive enough to suppose that ordained ministers are tax exempt. The result has been for some a sad awakening. They were subjected to excessive fines which so burdened and distressed them that in one or two cases which have come to our attention, they never fully recovered from the blow. A minister should not only have a record of his regular income, but he should keep an account of such income that comes to him through weddings, funerals, etc.

Others have failed to secure income tax exemption for their churches, which makes it impossible for donors to get credit for their gifts to the church. A state charter alone does not give this exemption. Their failure has caused some parishioners to lose hundreds of dollars. It would only be natural for them to conclude that their pastor was not a good businessman.

Still others have neglected such a simple step as providing fire or theft insurance on property that belonged to the church. The Scriptures enjoin us to "be diligent in business," and failure to heed this injunction may result in a preacher's suffering reverses that can seriously set him back in his ministry. By not complying with this one simple Scriptural command, some ministers have been greatly handicapped in fulfilling their call.

THE DANGER OF "GIMMICKS"

A minister who goes in for gimmicks will soon earn for himself a reputation that is by no means flattering. Gimmicks which included relics, bones, holy water, indulgences, etc., cursed the Medieval Church. They were widely used at that time as money-raising devices designed to appeal to people's ignorance and superstition. Today certain preachers are resorting to gimmicks to entice people to part with their money.

Let us say first, however, that there should be a clear distinction made between that which is legitimate and that which is not. Some opposers of apostolic ministry have declared that the sending out of prayer cloths is a gimmick. This of course is a serious error. There is definite Scriptural authority for sending out handkerchiefs or cloths which have been prayed over to sick persons (Acts 19:11-12). It is possible for healing virtue to be imparted from a cloth just as it passed from the garment of Christ to the afflicted person.

What we are referring to as gimmicks is the use of articles that purport to have some mysterious power or supposed virtue in them —a sort of charm or fetish—the use of which has no Scriptural foundation. These are analogous to the "strange fire" which was offered by Dathan and Abiram, sons of Aaron, divinely appointed priests, but who came under the judgment of God.

What are some of these gimmicks? The number apparently is endless, for new ones are heard of frequently. The partial list includes such things as follows: a "blessed purse" that causes money to multiply "supernaturally"; the "gift" of prosperity; "magic pictures" in which the image reappears after the person has closed his eyes (the eye when closed normally retains a reversed image); a special "prayer carpet"; "holy oil" or "holy water" that is supposed to carry a special virtue; cloths which "supernaturally" change color; "blessed nails"; "blessed pictures"; "blessed sawdust" on which an angel is supposed to have walked; a barrel of water in which an angel comes down and "troubles it"; "bottled demons," etc. These are only a few of the long list of gimmicks which have been offered to the public.

The Reformation actually had its beginning when Martin Luther became convinced that all the gimmicks the church used—the relics, the saints' bones, splinters from the "true cross," etc.—were phony and had no virtue. May God help the minister to abide in the simplicity and purity of the gospel and not attempt to mislead people with such things.

WRONG METHODS OF MONEY RAISING

All of us know that money is a necessary commodity in the kind of civilization in which we live. It is an important element in promoting Christian work. Its availability to a considerable extent governs the scope of our activities. It is, therefore, natural that a minister looks for ways and means by which he can secure necessary funds for the work that he feels called to do.

But here lurks many pitfalls in which the unwary may stumble. The line between the permissible and the objectionable is sometimes very thin. Some men have raised hundreds of thousands of dollars for missions, and their work is to be highly praised. Others have raised comparatively insignificant amounts, and the manner in which it was done or the way they used it, has called forth strong condemnation.

If people are told that the money is to be used for a certain purpose, and it is spent largely for other things, such as for promotion, then it is being raised under false pretenses. This is a sore point. Certainly there are costs in raising missionary money. Anyone who says otherwise doesn't speak the truth. But if the greater proportion of the funds so raised are used for overhead, then something is wrong.

Some men are careless in keeping records of the funds they handle. They fail to recognize that they have a responsibility to the public to show that they have been faithful stewards in discharging their obligations and keeping faith with their donors.

51

Operating a missionary program requires offices, an experienced staff, equipment, etc. It is very easy for overhead to eat up a large part of the missionary funds. For this reason no man should enter into an ambitious missionary program without the clear leading of God. A good test by which one can determine whether a program has God's favor upon it or not is whether a substantial part of the funds raised gets to the field.

The manner of taking offerings in a campaign is extremely important. If every service or a considerable number of services is occupied with a lengthy appeal for large offerings, the effect upon the people of the community is likely to be unfavorable. The ministers so engaged will soon be regarded as employed mainly in money raising. Worse, the people will become accustomed to giving only under high pressure. Money has to be raised, but this should be done at times especially designated for that purpose.

There should be a sensitivity to the feelings of the congregation on these matters. Certainly prolonged and continuous money raising is sure to result in severe reaction.

SOME BECOME SIDETRACKED ON A "DOCTRINAL HOBBY"

Some ministers fail because they become sidetracked on a "hobby." We are not referring to those who fall into deep error or heresy on which we need not comment, but rather to good men who take off into doctrinal sidelines, which are really out of the mainstream of the gospel message.

To make our point clear let us give a few examples: One evangelist showed unusual promise until he got involved in fighting a certain religion. Few people are helped by having their church savagely attacked even if they are aware of its errors. There are times when it may be necessary to point out the errors of a system, but generally speaking a direct attack on a church only arouses animosity and makes its people less receptive to the truth. A contentious spirit is not the spirit of Christianity. Paul tells us that we are to pray and make intercession "that we may lead a quiet and peaceable life in all godliness and honesty" (I Tim. 2:2).

Certain ministers stray into some prophetic novelty. Perhaps it has an element of truth; possibly it has error. What we do refer to, however, is the emphasis some are inclined to put on their "pet" doctrine or teaching. They get so carried away with it that it becomes a "hobby" with them. The prophetic field requires years of study, and it is advisable for the average minister not to get too far out on a limb on that subject.

Church history gives us a sad account of doctrinal controversies which were irrelevant to the mainstream of the gospel message. For example, there have been over the centuries at least a score of life-and-death struggles over such a simple matter as water baptism. Now water baptism is of great importance, but contention over it is not (Read I Cor. 1:11-17). Nevertheless, fierce controversies have raged over infant baptism, baptismal regeneration, whether the person should be sprinkled, poured, or immersed, whether a man should be rebaptized, whether in still or running water —disputes regarding the qualifications of the man who baptizes— the list is endless.

It is said that in one instance men argued hotly over the question of how many devils could dance on the point of a needle! The sad truth is that when men or a denomination go overboard on a sideline, their usefulness to God has to a large part been lost. Unfortunately, they are usually the last ones to be aware of this.

SOME FAIL BECAUSE THEY DO NOT STUDY

"Study to shew thyself approved unto God, a workman that needeth not to be ashamed, rightly dividing the word of truth" (II Tim. 2:15).

It is true that some men spend years seeking to add one degree upon another and yet remain spiritually barren in their souls. They have much in their heads, but little in their hearts. Because such cases occur, there is a tendency by some to downgrade the value of an education. This, however, is wrong. Education, spirituality, and a supernatural ministry should be compatible. Although it is more important to have religion in the heart than in the head, still it is better to have it both places.

Every minister who is a member of the body of Christ needs the inspiration and stimulation that comes from being exposed to other ministries. Elisha "poured water on the hands of Elijah" before he received the double-portion ministry. Joshua spent 40 years as an assistant to Moses before he became the great captain to lead the children of Israel into Canaan.

It is obvious that some ministers do not rise above mediocrity because they do not replenish their spiritual storehouse from which they must feed their people. They have not disciplined themselves to regular study. Consequently, they have little that is new and fresh to offer their congregations.

The Holy Spirit is the source of the anointing, but He can only anoint what the minister has gathered into his storehouse. The servant of God should continue his studies throughout life.

SOME MISS GOD BECAUSE THEY LET DOWN ON THEIR PENTECOSTAL TESTIMONY

Essentially the Pentecostal ministry is distinguished by its position that the supernatural gifts of the apostolic age were to continue down through the centuries, that the baptism in the Holy Spirit which Christ promised to His disciples was to be experienced by believers in all generations, that the ministry of divine healing was to continue, that the gifts of the Holy Spirit were to find manifestation throughout the entire age.

Nevertheless, to enter into supernatural ministry costs something. It is not always an easy road. It may seem easier to practice rituals or externals of religion than to pay the price of the supernatural ministry.

The book of Joshua closes with the significant statement that Joshua's generation, and the one which survived him and had witnessed the wonders of the Lord, continued faithful to God (Joshua 24:31). But the inspired writer adds that it was in the third generation after the spiritual outpouring that apostasy set in. This occurred about sixty years after the Exodus. Now we note that a similar period of time, sixty years, has elapsed since the great outpouring of the Spirit took place in Los Angeles and spread around the world. Today we see deadly undercurrents at work to produce a declension in apostolic ministry. History is repeating itself.

God has called us to a work that will take everything we have. We must be willing to risk all for Christ. There will be steps to take requiring sheer faith. There will be times when we will have to take a stand that may be unpopular. A minister may be tempted to go against his better judgment and "play it safe" for the sake of what appears to be security for himself and his family. When a preacher surrenders his convictions for what seems a more practical course, he has chosen what is called "the world's slow stain."

These are days when there is a temptation to move with the tide, to remain silent when one should stand up and be counted. Thus do spiritual movements cool off and depart from their initial fervor. As Jude said in his day, "Certain men have crept in unaware" with their perverse doctrines, and those who should contend for the faith hold their peace. In other words they do not want to get involved. They are satisfied to follow the herd. But in pleasing men we may fail to please God. In a search for material security we may miss God's security.

We recall a man who had achieved a high position in his movement, but when the revival came and he should have thrown his weight behind it (for it was the very thing he had preached for many years), he instead allowed himself to become identified with those who took a stand against it. Perhaps he felt he had some excuse. There were things that happened in the revival that deserved criticism and required correction, but the opposers he joined were not only against the excesses, they were against the revival.

The hour came when a fatal sickness struck this good man down. When the attending physicians said, "There is no hope," whom did he call to pray for him? The critics? No! We do not call for critics to pray the prayer of faith when we have a desperate need. We call for those who believe in the power of God. But alas, in this case, it was too late.

Had this gifted man stood firm for what he taught and believed many years, there is every reason to believe that he would have had many more years of fruitful ministry. He was a good man and could have been a great encouragement to those who were launching out into apostolic ministry. But one cannot be swept along with the Phariseeic tide and then have faith for a miracle in the hour of need.

FAILURE TO RECOGNIZE THE HEADSHIP OF CHRIST

"In the multitude of counsellors there is safety" (Prov. 24:6). God has used organizations and movements, though imperfect, to further His work. There is certainly nothing wrong in men working together. Organizations are working agreements between men whereby they can accomplish together what they could not do as well apart. But in the providence of God, Christ must always be the head, free to lead and guide His people. There are areas in which organizations must not tread. History shows the sad results when this caution is ignored.

There must always be room for Holy Ghost initiative. A man should be free to be led by the Spirit to the place and kind of service to which God has called him. Of course, other men may suggest and advise. It is certainly not against divine will for His ministers to counsel with one another. Often the mind of God is found in that way (Read Acts 15). But in the ultimate sense, a man must be led by the Spirit in his work for God.

It must be understood, however, that God never asks his servants to do anything contrary to ethics. The Lord would never ask any man to enter another man's church, to accept his hospitality, and then draw off members to start a congregation of his own. Nor does it look good in the eyes of the community to build a church in the same block or in the immediate proximity of another of like faith.

But now consider the other side of the problem. When the Lord leads a man to establish a work in a new city, it is probable that he will find other churches of the same faith in that community. Some of the people from these churches may visit the services of the new minister. Human nature being what it is, it is not unlikely that some of the preachers of these churches will be unhappy about what to them is "competition." It is here that danger arises. These ministers may use ecclesiastical pressure to try to usher the man out of the community. This is a most mischievous thing, for it is usurping the headship of Christ. The man who allows such threats to interfere with what he knows is divine leading may make a serious mistake—one that could affect his ministry for years to come. God help us to keep from infringing on the headship of Christ.

A LET-DOWN IN SPIRITUALITY

Some ministers who have shown great promise fail and have even left the ministry. It is not always easy to put one's finger on the cause. Perhaps they have had considerable success as preachers, and may have succeeded in building up a large congregation, but in helping their members become real Christians they have not succeeded.

It is not unlikely that such a minister has neglected his prayer closet. In other cases the answer may be that the man allowed worldliness to creep into his life, although he would probably resent such a charge.

All ministers need some kind of recreation, but woe to him that chooses the wrong kind. Some preachers get into the habit of relaxing by reading cheap literature. Others stay up regularly to see the late-late shows, which any person if he is honest must admit as being worse than trash. In fact more and more late showings on television appeal to debased tastes. He that is a willing witness to entertainment of that nature for relaxation cannot come away unsullied.

Some ministers become known as patrons of the theater and

other forms of worldly entertainment. Such persons are bound to suffer loss of reputation in the eyes of spiritual people.

A man of God who has been given the task of providing food for God's sheep cannot himself feast with the dead. It is no wonder that he who follows this course will in time find less and less appetite for spiritual things.

The apostle's advice who said, "Touch not; taste not; handle not; which are all to perish with the using," is still good (Col. 2:21). "Wherefore come out from among them, and be ye separate, saith the Lord, and touch not the unclean thing; and I will receive you" (II Cor. 6:17).

When we consider the matter of worldliness, we of course enter upon controversial ground. Who will admit that he is worldly? Yet history abounds with evidence that when the church deteriorated and lost its vision and power, its clergymen had first become worldly and materially minded. What is worldliness? Essentially it is a desire to be in conformity with the world. Paul warns against this in Romans 12:2 "And be not conformed to this world; but be ye transformed by the renewing of your mind, that ye may prove what is that good and acceptable, and perfect will of God." John described worldliness as yielding to the "lust of the flesh and the lust of the eyes and the pride of life." "Love not the world," he says," neither the things that are in the world. If any man love the world, the love of the Father is not in him. For all that is in the world, the lust of the flesh, and the lust of the eyes, and the pride of life, is not of the Father, but is of the world. And the world passeth away, and the lust thereof: but he that doeth the will of God abideth for ever" (I John 2:15-17).

James makes a stronger statement. We are espoused unto Christ; therefore, if our affections are transferred to this world, we are said to be spiritual adulterers and adulteresses. "Ye adulterers and adulteresses, know ye not that the friendship of the world is enmity with God? Whosoever therefore will be a friend of the world is the enemy of God" (James 4:4).

That the trend in the church in the last days would be toward materialism was clearly anticipated by Jesus in His message to the last of the Seven Churches of Revelation—the Laodicean Church (Read Rev. 3:15-21).

There are things a Christian should not do and places he should not go. But if the heart is worldly, all arguments fail. He who is in tune with the world will be happy only in worldly things. If by any means you convince him that certain things are not Christlike, he is only convinced against his will. He may be a reformed man, but not a transformed one. Yet if he can be infused with a holy love for Christ, the things of the world will of themselves fade away. He will be eager to live as close to Christ as he can, and as Paul of old he will say,

> "Yea doubtless, and I count all things but loss for the excellency of the knowledge of Christ Jesus my Lord: for whom I have suffered the loss of all things, and do count them but dung, that I may win Christ" (Phil. 3:8).

SOME ENTER THE MINISTRY BEFORE THEY ARE READY

It is obvious that the greatest of care should be exercised in the licensing and ordaining of ministers. Sometimes a pastor will be subjected to pressure to have a certain individual licensed or ordained. Although he may have misgivings, he yields to the pressure. Then he discovers that the man, after his elevation, fails to measure up. Sometimes such a person ceases to be of value in his home church or anywhere else.

Many things should be taken into consideration before a man is licensed or ordained to the ministry. First, does he have a definite call? Second, has he prepared himself for the ministry as the apostle Paul enjoined? "Study to shew thyself approved unto God, a workman that needeth not to be ashamed, rightly dividing the word of truth" (II Tim. 2:15). Whichever way a man gets his knowledge of the Scriptures, whether at a school or studying at home, he must get it. Nothing is more embarrassing to the ministry than to hear a rambling harangue by an ignorant preacher.

Third, has his life, as a Christian measured up? Even deacons are required to be blameless (I Tim. 3:10). Fourth, has he a real compassion for souls, or is he merely desiring a title, or wanting to escape the draft, or for some other similar motive? These things, as well as others, need to be taken into consideration before a man is set into the ministry.

It should not be necessary to add that a young man ought to be licensed before he is ordained. There should be a period in which the candidate has opportunity to prove his ministry, that he has the qualities that will make him stick to the task, regardless of the disappointments and trials that may be his lot.

Certainly a man before he is licensed should have a definite ministry of the Word. He should be more than an exhorter. He must be able to rightly divide the word of truth and apply it to practical living. We thank God that there are those who have been truly called to the ministry. Often they have a difficult time getting started. The question is often asked as to how they may best find an opening for their calling. To this we say: that you go to the poor and to the underprivileged. They will receive you and give you an open door. If you succeed in blessing them there will be plenty of calls for your ministry elsewhere.

CHAPTER 11

The Prize of the High Calling

Most books written for ministers deal only with this life. The Scriptures go further. They reveal that there is a continuity of purpose in the divine program between this world and the one to come. In other words this life is but a preparation for another. One of the great truths of the New Testament is that there is not only salvation to be accepted as a gift, but there is in addition a *prize to be won*. Of this the apostle Paul speaks in Philippians 3:13-14:

> "Brethren, I count not myself to have apprehended: but this one thing I do, forgetting those things which are behind, and reaching forth unto those things which are before, I press toward the mark for the prize of the high calling of God in Christ Jesus."

Not all Christians or ministers realize that there is a prize to be gained. Notwithstanding there is a special reward promised to those who win the race. The rewards for service will be given at the time we stand before the judgment seat of Christ. That we all must appear before Him to give an account of deeds done in the body is a solemn matter for every believer to consider.

This judgment does not involve our salvation, but rather our reward. Everything in our life that we have done will be judged at that time—with the exception of our sins. Thank God these will have been judged beforehand in Christ! Blotted out, they will be remembered against us no more. Nevertheless, our works will be judged. Each act of our life has been recorded and will be weighed on the basis of whether we have labored because of love for our Lord or whether it has been done for self-glory and the praise of of men. Christ said, "Take heed that ye do not your alms before men to be seen of them: otherwise ye have no reward of your Father which is in heaven" (Matt. 6:1). The Pharisees did these things for that purpose, and of them Jesus said, "Verily I say unto you, They have their reward."

The words of Paul in I Cor. 3:13-15 are something every minister should give his most earnest attention. In these verses Paul speaks of a believer's works being tried by fire to test whether they are of gold, silver, and precious stones, or of wood, hay, or stubble.

"Every man's work shall be made manifest: for the day shall declare it, because it shall be revealed by fire; and the fire shall try every man's work of what sort it is. If any man's work abide which he hath built thereupon, he shall receive a reward. If any man's work shall be burned, he shall suffer loss: but he himself shall be saved; yet so as by fire" (I Cor. 3:13-15).

At that great day Christ will sit on His throne and judge the earth and His people. That which is done to be seen of men or for human glory will be judged as hay, wood, and stubble. These works will be burned up, and for such persons there will be no reward. That which has been done for God's glory and in compassion for the lost will stand the test and for these a reward shall be given.

After the judgment at the tribunal of Christ, each man will be given his position of rank for which he has fitted himself. In this world men achieve position largely on the basis of native ability and talent. But in the world to come a man will be promoted on the basis of his faithfulness to the task that was given him on earth, be it large or small. Thus did the Lord commend the faithful servant who had earned only two talents, the same as He did the one who had gained five.

"His lord said unto him, Well done, good and faithful servant; thou hast been faithful over a few things, I will make thee ruler over many things: enter thou into the joy of thy Lord" (Matt. 25:23).

There will be great differences in rank and position in the world to come. The Parable of the Pounds shows this difference in position. When the Lord passed out the rewards, He gave to one, authority over ten cities, to another, five cities, etc. (Luke 19:11-19). There will be some who will reign as kings; others will be given responsible positions but of lesser authority. All who are redeemed will receive eternal life, as did the thief on the cross; but not all will win a reward.

Paul hints again and again of the prize that he himself was seeking. The supreme reward is to achieve a position close to Christ, even as the first-fruits unto God are said to "follow the Lamb whithersoever He goeth" (Rev. 14:1-5).

All will see Him; all shall be known of Him; but there will be those who are closer to Him than others. These are they who will rule and reign with Christ. All will serve Him, for the world to come is not a place of inactivity. The saints are not translated merely to play harps or wave palm branches. They will do that— but they will also participate in dethroning Satan from the heavenlies and setting up of Christ's kingdom on earth for the Millennium (Rev. 12:7-14). The warfare against Satan in the heavenlies is not restricted to angels. The saints of God are participating in the battle of the heavenlies now. After translation the battle will be consummated. Satan will be cast down on the earth and after that into the bottomless pit.

Today the call of the Bridegroom goes forth to His Bride. The Messianic psalm, Psalm 45, tells us about it:

> "Hearken, O daughter, and consider, and incline thine ear; forget also thine own people, and thy father's house; So shall the king greatly desire thy beauty: for he is thy Lord; and worship thou him" (Psa. 45:10-11).

This is a call not all will hear. They are not tuned in closely enough. But Paul felt the call, and it became so great an obsession that he considered "all things loss" that he might win Christ. All the hardships of the ministry he counted negligible, as a mere inconvenience. All other goals paled into insignificance as he viewed the prize set before him.

Beyond the Millennium is the ages of ages. Paul says, "That in the ages to come he might show the exceeding riches of his grace in his kindness toward us through Christ Jesus" (Eph. 2:7). We can only have a faint idea of the glories that are to be revealed or the greatness of the divine plan which will expand out into the infinite universe in the millenniums which are to come. "Known unto God are all His works from the beginning of the world." But there will be many glorious surprises for us. Of what is to be revealed in the future the Scriptures give us only a bare hint. Our finite minds do not have the capacity to take all this in. This much we should know, what we do today and our faithfulness to what God has called us to do, will largely determine our place and position in the eternity which is to be revealed. Therefore, as heirs of this great inheritance let us press forward toward the prize of the high calling so that when we come to the end of the way, we as the apostle Paul will be able to say,

> "I have fought a good fight, I have finished my course, I have kept the faith: Henceforth there is laid up for me a crown of righteousness, which the Lord, the righteous judge, shall give me at that day: and not to me only, but unto all them also that love his appearing" (II Tim. 4:7-8).

CHAPTER 12

The Ministry of A Pastor

"And he gave some . . . pastors" (Ephes. 4:11).

Much of what is written in our previous volume on the Pentecostal ministry has more or less application to all ministers. In this chapter, however, we shall consider specifically the work of a pastor. Truly the office of a pastor is a high calling, and he that is successful in it has a great reward awaiting him. Who is the one that is asked for when illness comes or misfortune strikes, or trouble befalls a family? Who is the one expected to comfort the bereaved when death visits a home but the man who stands in the pulpit and gives forth the word of life?

To be a successful pastor does not require extraordinary brilliance, but it does demand certain qualifications. He is first of all the shepherd of the sheep, and as such is God's representative. The New Testament speaks of him as an elder, a bishop, an overseer of God's work (Acts 20:28; I Pet. 2:25; I Pet. 5:1). He is a ruler of God's household and exercises authority (I Tim. 3:5; 5:17, Heb. 13:17), but not as an overlord of God's heritage (I Pet. 5:3).

Many and varied are his duties. He must minister meat in due season to his household (Matt. 24:45). As an intercessor and priest he stands between the living and the dead. As a shepherd he is guardian of the flock and knows each of his sheep by name. He watches for the little foxes which spoil the vines, and protects the lambs from wolves that hover about ever seeking to attack the unwary one which wanders too far from the flock.

The ministry of a pastor is considerably different from that of an evangelist. Nevertheless, to a degree he does the work of an evangelist. Every day he must let his light shine. His life is to be an example to his people. He must be careful of every act, knowing whatever he does will add or detract in some way to his influence in the community.

The pastor's ministry is of a varied nature and calls for the very best that is within him. His sermons must be carefully prepared with the purpose of reaching the hearts of people. He must preach the truth, but it must be done acceptably. His sermons must be Bible-oriented, yet relevant to the issues of the day. A test of his effectiveness is whether or not souls are saved. Being successful in winning new converts, however, is not enough. The pastor must lead them on step by step into the Holy Spirit baptism and into a full knowledge of the truth of the gospel. He must watch carefully, lest some backslide and fall away. And above all this he must ever work for unity and harmony among his people.

Christ said to His disciples, "Feed my lambs." That means that the pastor must constantly labor to build a strong Sunday morning Bible school. He must labor to hold the students when they reach the ages of 14-16—that period when youth is most apt to be lost to the church. He should encourage the development of a strong young people's society. He must understand and secure an "empathy" with them if he is to be a successful pastor.

An enlightened pastor will have a strong interest in missions. The church is the home base for evangelizing the world. Failure to develop an interest among his congregation in missionary endeavor is a fatal weakness. A church which has little concern for those who live in heathen darkness is guilty of the most flagrant selfishness.

All in all the work of the pastor involves a wide range of responsibilities and obligations. His task would be overwhelming were it not that he is a co-laborer with Christ who said, "My yoke is easy and my burden is light."

The man of God must be impartial. He will not cater to the rich or to the influential. He must as Paul be all things to all people that he might win some. He will not fail to rebuke open sin as the apostle directed (I Tim. 5:20). He will radiate cheer and optimism, but not condescend to jesting and foolish talking (Ephes. 5:4). Yet he should avoid the sanctimoniousness of the Pharisee. He will show enthusiasm in his work. He cannot rise or fall with the daily fluctuations. And if the day comes when disaster strikes his community, he will be a tower of strength to his people.

A shepherd of God's sheep must be of unimpeachable character. Like shepherd, like sheep. The pastor invariably leaves the stamp of his own spirituality upon his people. He must practice what he preaches. In all things he is an example to his flock and to the community where he lives (I Tim. 4:12; Titus 2:7). A pastor, therefore, will avoid the appearance of evil. There are always gossipy tongues who are ready to pass on some choice morsel at the barest hint of a pastor's indiscretion.

A minister should be courteous (I Pet. 3:8, Rom. 2:10). By nature he is warm and approachable. He will show a sincere interest in the welfare of the members of his flock. Their interests are his. Christ mingled with the people, so likewise the pastor will keep close to his sheep.

The pastor must show that he is a good businessman before he leads his people into undertakings involving heavy financial responsibilities. An autocratic spirit is sure to result in unfavorable reaction and can even bring about rebellion in the congregation. When one is instituting a new program it is wise to wait until there is a general unanimity. When a sizeable minority is against the program, it can cause real trouble for the pastor. Peace and harmony in the church is of great price, and it can be destroyed by a man who rides roughshod over everyone who does not see things his way. A stubborn dictatorial spirit does not inspire loyalty among the people.

A wise pastor puts his people to work. As the old saying goes, "The devil finds work for idle hands." As a leader he should ever be on the alert to find suitable tasks for his members. He should as far as possible take advantage of the talent among the members of the congregation. People who are busy do not have time on their hands to criticize and find fault with the pastor.

We have seen some pastors busy serving as choreboys for their church. While a minister should if necessary show that he can work with his hands, as for example when some construction is being done on the church and funds are low, yet his time is worth far more to the church in visiting and reaching new people. Even a few extra families brought in will more than compensate financially for what a pastor can do in the way of manual labor, not to speak of what a pastor can do for people spiritually.

A minister should be punctual. He keeps his appointments. He carefully arranges his time to use it to the best advantage. In his visitation with the members of his flock he must not seem hurried; yet there is a right moment to terminate his visit.

A minister is sometimes wrongly accused, misunderstood, or misrepresented. In most cases it is best to overlook what has been said. A man who is super-sensitive to every adverse criticism will not get far in the ministry. Nonetheless, let him be careful that his actions are not worthy of censure. For example, dabbling on the side in business ventures is not only usually unproductive but invites criticism. Naturally we are not referring to a situation in which the congregation is small, and the pastor must work for a time with his hands. A man is responsible for providing for his household, but let him flee money-making for money's sake.

A pastor should from the beginning learn the life of faith. In the ultimate, he must look to God and not to man. God has promised to supply all our needs. We should remember the words of the psalmist, "The Lord is my shepherd; I shall not want." A minister should beware of temptation to borrow from those of his congregation. This fault has hurt many preachers who have gotten themselves into a situation in which they could not repay their members.

A minister must take his religion with him into his home. Of course his first task is to find the right helpmate. While there are many snares waiting for the unmarried pastor, a wrong marriage will prove to be a steel trap. To a large extent the wife holds the success of her husband in her hands. One fault of some wives is that they become retailers of gossip. Some who have a sharp tongue can nullify all the good their husbands can do. And yet a wise and prudent wife can be an inestimable asset to a man of God. When a man goes through adverse circumstances, how it strengthens him to have a faithful companion at his side giving encouragement and support.

A pastor must remember that his health is an important factor to the success of his ministry. There are times when he must break away from the daily routine for a season of relaxation. The occasional vacation is not a waste of time by any means. Jesus called His disciples apart for periods of rest (Mark 6:31). Rest is not a luxury; it is a necessity.

Preaching the Word of course is at the top of the list of the responsibilities of a pastor. It should, however, be applicable to everyday living. Christ drew largely upon His observations and experiences in daily life to illustrate His teachings. The minister should be constantly on the alert for illustrations and material for his sermons. In his work of visitation, the pastor gets to understand the needs of his people. As he hears their troubles he learns their special problems and acquires their point of view. Thus he is constantly gathering sermon material which will be of genuine interest and help to his people. Of course he should refrain from using any illustration that might embarrass a member of his congregation.

A preacher should be an extensive reader. A major part of his studies should center on the Scriptures. Nevertheless, he should not neglect the writings of other men of God. As he reads, it is good for him to practice underlining striking paragraphs, marking any illustrations which especially appeal to him. Some preachers have no windows in their sermons. This is a serious mistake. People listen and absorb the truth more readily when it is illustrated. That was Christ's favorite method of teaching.

Advertising has a place in the church. If it has something worthwhile to offer, people should know about it. One excellent method of keeping in touch with the community is to secure the names and addresses of visitors who attend the services. When the church has special services, announcements can then be sent to them. People who have attended services once are apt to come again if an invitation is extended to them.

A pastor should be careful not to build his attendance on sensationalism. In the long run, audiences will be more consistent if the work done is of a solid Bible-oriented nature. Advertising should be used but not overdone. W. B. Riley tells of a certain hand bill advertising the speaker which read as follow:

> "Mr. - - - - - is a man of unusual brain power and spiritual illumination. He combines in a rare degree the exactness of the scientist, the idealism of the philosopher, the vision of a seer, and the truth of a Bible student. The lectures are considered among the greatest productions of the age in which we live. A volume could be filled with commendatory letters from ministers, educators, and people in all walks of life ... Simply great; no other words to use ... Most dramatic speaker in America ... A fearless crusader ... Always draws big crowds ... He is a Kansas cyclone ... His lectures are worth $5,000 to me."

A thoughtful person could have only one conclusion: that the handbill was modeled after the showbills of P. T. Barnum.

An advertisement should be carefully prepared. One newspaper ad that came to our notice was indiscriminately filled with items that had been jammed together without regard to context. A quite unintentional effect was produced by two lines placed one after the other. They read: "Do you know the devil talks to people today? . . . Come and hear H............."

Delaying the hour of opening a meeting is indefensible. Sometimes services get off to a poor start because the preacher sermonizes while he is giving the announcements. The speaker of the evening should get the pulpit while the minds of the people are still fresh.

Another grave mistake is failure of a preacher to stop when his discourse is ended. Some speakers after dwelling on their last point say, "Now in conclusion," then in a few minutes, "Finally, my brethren," and "Now one last thought." It is said that fast moving trains blow their whistles three times before they come to a stop, but some preachers blow theirs half a dozen times and keep on going!

The purpose of a sermon will determine the manner of its conclusion. If evangelistic, the net should be drawn in. If the message is to Christians, a call to consecration may be appropriate. If on healing, a prayer for the sick should follow. If for missionary purposes, an offering is in order.

A pastor should be careful not to have too many boards. They will tend to overlap and thereby conflict. A single church board in most cases should be sufficient. One thing to watch out for is not to have several weak members on the board and one strong one. This tends to a one-man rule. A pastor at election time should never speak against the man he does not want elected. He may, however, speak quietly and favorably of those he wants. And above all have the people pray that the right ones will be chosen. A pastor should not fear having a board. A well-constituted advisory board is the pastor's protection and provides him with advice and assistance in carrying on the many duties of the church.

A pastor should think through his church problems. He is in a place where he can survey the whole field and it is to his interest to see that the proper decisions are made. He ought not to expect others who have not had time to give serious consideration to church problems to take the initiative in formulating plans. The pastor is and should be the leader. He must not dominate, but he should lead.

All churches will have problems at times—occasionally a really serious one. A church problem is not necessarily a menace. But to escape from evil results, it must be dealt with properly. Church troubles if they linger do not leave the pastor unscathed. For one thing, he should do nothing to provoke or stir up problems. An indolent pastor, one who is careless, one who rests upon his oars, is certain to come in for criticism. A pastor's wife must learn to hold her tongue. Other women can talk, but what the pastor's wife says goes further and creates more trouble than the tongues of a dozen others; hence she cannot afford this "luxury."

69

If the trouble is minor, it may be best to ignore it. Many disturbances die of themselves. Some preachers, if they hear a word of criticism, fly after the folk who made it. They will insist on proof and in some cases even demand a trial. There is an old saying that a preacher, guilty or innocent, is dead before the trial starts. It is good advice not to fight with everyone who comes around with a chip on his shoulder.

We cannot here go into the subject of church problems. If there is some misunderstanding between brethren, the Scriptures provide a way of settling it. Seek reconciliation. Failing that, there is still a way to deal with troublemakers.

The average church trouble exists because there is not enough prayer. People want to do things their way instead of God's way. Experience proves that the power of prayer usually overcomes the opposition. Read the story of Daniel, Chapter 6.

We are to trust in the Lord rather than in councils, secret sessions, or maneuvering. The pastor who does his duty, commits his way to God, keeps the spirit of prayer going in his church, will usually come out unscathed, even as did Daniel, and in the end will witness the confusion and overthrow of his enemies.

THE MINISTER'S WIFE

A minister's wife who proves worthy of her calling can almost double her husband's usefulness. If she falls short of the mark through lack of consecration or ability she may drive him into secular work. Like her husband she should have a call from God.

Her first duty of course is to make her husband's home life comfortable and to free him from domestic cares. But her responsibilities go far beyond the home. A pastor's wife should by all means be a warm, outgoing individual. Some women feel that they can take their particular problems to another woman more easily than to the pastor. Therefore, the wife should be approachable and qualified to give counsel to those women of the congregation who come to her for help.

In smaller churches she may be needed to lead the choir or head the missionary society. In a larger church where there are others who are qualified for such tasks, it is probable that she can do more good by encouraging them to fill those places.

There are differences of opinion as to whether or not a pastor's wife should accompany her husband on calls. In some cases it is obviously advisable. Yet there is a danger that the calls made by both husband and wife will take on the aspect of a social visit. Two persons usually do not receive the sort of confidences that the minister would if he were alone.

Obviously unless a pastor's wife has help with the housework, she cannot regularly accompany him on his calls. If she visits some and not others, she may be accused of playing favorites. There is also danger in starting something that cannot be kept up, especially if the church is large and has many members. Nevertheless, despite what has been said, the writer found that when he took over the pastorate of a small church, the help of his wife in visitation was of great assistance in the rapid growth of the membership of the church. Moreover, because she was active in this way we found it easy to get other members enthusiastic in the work of visitation.

Certainly a pastor's wife has many fields of usefulness, especially in the counselling of women and girls. There are times when they need intimate advice that the pastor cannot give. When a tempted or erring sister comes to her, she must not appear shocked but be able to give her loving and compassionate guidance. A wise pastor's wife can be an inestimable asset to her husband in helping to bind up the wounds of broken hearts.

Andrew W. Blackwood says in summing up the place of a pastor's wife:

> "The most immediate privilege of the pastor's wife is to make her husband happy. The best place to let her light shine is through the windows of a happy home; by making the house neat and attractive; by planning wholesome meals, not too heavy; by keeping him from overindulgence of appetite; by rearing several children aright; by talking over any problems on which he wants light; and refraining from being 'boss' of the congregation. She may be the power behind the throne, but she ought not to be the big stick. Love works best by indirection."

The number of pastors with domestic difficulties presents a situation more serious than is commonly supposed. Certainly the happiest and most useful ministers are those whose wives have provided them with a congenial home atmosphere.

All conduct in the home should be based on the laws of common courtesy. A great deal of marital friction comes because one mate takes the other for granted and becomes discourteous.

Naturally the other person will resent such conduct, and this can result in a rift.

A pastor's wife can be of help in the matter of her husband's sermons. She can aid him more by intelligent praise than by criticism. She should never "sit in the seat of the scornful" but rather be in the cheering section. By praising her husband for the good points of his message, she may be able without deflating him, to point out little annoying mannerisms or the mispronunciation of certain words. After a minister preaches a sermon he needs encouragement not criticism. It is not unusual for a preacher to feel depleted or even wretched after he has finished his message, and he doesn't need more "cold water" poured on him. Later she can point out something that would be helpful, but she should do it tactfully and with love. Nothing could be worse than for a minister to have a nagging critic in his home.

One of the circumstances which is important to the wife is the location of the parsonage. Often the pastor lives next door to the church. In some ways this is a convenience. But in other ways it can be a disadvantage. When the parsonage is next door to the church it is very easy for folk to drop in at any time, either to visit or to talk on trivial matters. The wife may have to put up with bores by the hour.

Yet if the pastor lives too far from the church, he may lose much time in commuting. Some ministers spend an hour or more a day in going back and forth to their study. This loss of time is doubled when he has services in the evening. Perhaps the most ideal place is for the pastor to live within a few blocks of the church. In case a car is not available, any member of the family can walk to the church. They are far enough away so that they can enjoy some home life and yet near enough that they can be in close touch with all that goes on.

CHAPTER 13

The Ministry of An Evangelist

"And he gave some . . . evangelists" (Ephes. 4:11).

It has often been said that it would be good if every evangelist served a while as a pastor, and every pastor was for a time an evangelist. Unfortunately, this is not always possible.

Most pastors call evangelists regularly to their churches. Some, perhaps as a result of an unfortunate experience, reject the use of the evangelistic ministry. This we believe is a great mistake. An important part of the success of any special meeting, however, is in having the right man at the right time. A big name evangelist may not always be the answer. To reject the ministry of all evangelists is to deprive the people of one of the gifts that God has placed in the church. Some disparagingly refer to evangelists as "professionals." Nevertheless, there is no more reason to speak of professional evangelists than of professional pastors. There may be some of both, but they are not peculiar to one group. An evangelist, nonetheless, is in a position to have more criticism directed at him than a pastor. Often he is compelled to labor under extremely adverse conditions.

As a pastor for several years, I wish to say that the ministry of evangelism contributed very substantially to the growth of our church. We did, however, exercise special care in our selection of evangelists. There is not only the matter of securing the right man, but in choosing the right time for his coming. We found it helpful if we could size up the speaker beforehand and thus be better able to prepare the congregation for his particular type of ministry.

The first evangelist that we had in our pastorate was a man who literally "murdered" the king's English. Our congregation was not large, but it did include some who were teachers or who had a college education. Despite the evangelist's lack of polish I felt that he had the ministry the church needed at that time. We took the people into our confidence and prepared them for his coming by explaining that the man had an unusual anointing but that his English was probably not what they were used to. The people did receive the evangelist well, and I might say that the meeting gave us the breakthrough that we were looking for and needed. In two years' time the church grew from being one of the smallest to one of the largest in the district.

How do evangelism and revivals fit into the picture of the Christian ministry? The theory of revival is consistent with nature itself. Life has a tendency to ebb and flow rather than being sustained at one level. Springtime is a revival of nature. There are springtimes of divine visitation, when the Spirit arouses the spiritual lethargies of men. At such times a pastor may find it advantageous to secure the services of an outside speaker.

The Bible teaches and observation fully confirms it, that something has happened to human nature which gives it a strong predisposition to evil. There is a law of degeneracy in a man's nature that causes him to ignore God. Because of this tendency it is not surprising that his interests are occupied largely with material things. It is, therefore, understandable that the average man requires some powerful influence to arrest his attention sufficiently to make him willing to change his way of life.

And when an impression is made it needs to be repeated. Strong-minded and influential people at the beginning of a campaign may appear to show little interest in the salvation of their souls, but after hearing the gospel preached a number of times their impressions may deepen to the point at which they will make the all-important decision for Christ. The revival meeting furnishes the time and place for such to happen.

There are several factors operating to produce a spiritual atmosphere conducive to a man's making a favorable decision. The preaching plays a vital part, but that is not all. In the Welsh revival there was little preaching, but there was an impelling something that subdued the rebellious spirit and brought a deep conviction of sin. The music, the manifestation of personal concern, all have their share in producing this atmosphere; but more than anything else it is intercessory prayer and travail of soul that are most important.

The history of revival shows that wherever there have been unusual visitations of grace, there was first much agonizing travail of soul and earnest appeal to God for the salvation of the lost.

What about the character of the man that God chooses as an evangelist. He must be of sterling character, for he will be subjected to strong temptations. Nothing pleases the devil more than to have the appearance of evil magnified to the point at which it can ruin a man and his ministry. Therefore, it is imperative that the evangelist use the greatest caution in all his relations with the opposite sex or in his financial dealings.

A man who engages in evangelism successfully must be a man who knows how to pray. It is said that the apostle James at his death was found to have his knees calloused like a camel's knees because of so much kneeling.

An evangelist may speak strongly against evil and error, but he should never cruelly ridicule other denominations. Ridicule and scorn have no place in the ministry. The Word of God instructs, "If a man be overtaken in a fault, ye which are spiritual, restore such an one in the spirit of meekness..." (Gal. 6:1). An attitude of love and genuine concern should be manifested when delivering a message.

An evangelist should exercise due judgment in the matter of caring for his physical health. He should know the limitations of his strength and conduct his activities accordingly. Those who come to hear him expect him to be at his best. A man can go into the pulpit so tired that his message may weary the people instead of inspiring them. A common mistake is for evangelists to schedule their campaigns too close together. There needs to be at least brief periods of recuperation between meetings. When a minister goes beyond what his normal strength allows he draws on his reserve nervous energy which often requires a long time to be replenished. Some of the finest evangelists we have known by reason of ill-health have been forced to leave the field at the very height of their ministry. This to say the least, is tragic. God has spent years to prepare a man for a much needed ministry and then it is suddenly terminated. There is nothing that pleases the devil better than this.

The evangelist in his preaching should remember that a considerable proportion of his audience does not think profoundly. Some may have been on their feet all during the day and are too tired for deep intellectual effort. He, therefore, should not design his message for a few intellectuals, but should get down to earth and put the Bread of Life out where the common people can grasp it.

Another thing to remember is that each message should be prepared for a purpose. It should be aimed at reaching men's consciences. Paul's words made Felix tremble. The sermon, therefore, is not an end, but a means to an end.

An evangelist should not be afraid to use illustrations. They are the windows of his message. However, illustrations should not be used for their own sake; they are to illuminate the truth. Illustrations taken from daily life are generally more effective than those culled out of books that have been used over and over by other speakers.

And now a few words about promotion. Is it Scriptural for a church to advertise? Jesus said, "Neither do men light a candle and put it under a bushel." The gospel is what the people need most so they should know of it. Preaching to empty seats makes no converts, however good the sermon is.

But one should not advertise more than he can deliver. Sometimes ministers announce a catchy title and then fail to preach on the subject, or else what they say relates only remotely to it. An evangelist should be honest with the people, and never trick them in order to get a crowd.

Newspaper advertising is good, but it can be overdone. In many of the large campaigns with which the writer has been associated, we used comparatively little newspaper advertising; yet we filled the largest auditoriums. Word spread that miracles were taking place, and when the people came they were not disappointed. It is permissible to advertise that miracles are taking place, but in such case the evangelist must produce.

Much depends on the efforts made after the revival if the results are to be conserved. In a ministers' conference in a northern city some years ago, a certain pastor said that he did not believe in evangelists, since out of 103 names which had been given to his church in a previous campaign, only two were in active membership. But another pastor remarked, "That is very peculiar, for I received precisely the same number of names, and in looking over my church roll the other day I found that all of them except two are now consistent members of my church!"

The close of an evangelistic campaign is a crucial moment. Let those who labored during the revival be ever so zealous, yet if the work is not followed up, much of what has been accomplished will be lost. When Judas and Silas went to Antioch where there had been a mighty revival, we are told that they "exhorted the brethren with many words, and confirmed them" (Acts 15:32). The permanency of the work in a revival depends largely on the efforts of the pastor after the evangelist leaves. The fact is that many converts will slip back into their old life and be lost forever if the church does not carefully look after and nurture these babes in Christ.

We have heard the words, "We'll wait and see if they hold out," spoken by some in reference to new converts. Such an attitude is almost criminal, and in the sight of God it is a sin of unusual flagrance. If all members of the congregation should take such an attitude, the church would cease to grow. Just as physical life hangs in the balance with a new born babe, so spiritual life is even more delicate at its beginning. It is the business of the church to see that the new converts do hold out.

When the days of Judah's captivity drew near, the Spirit of the Lord spoke to the shepherds of Israel saying, "Where is the flock that was given thee, thy beautiful flock? What wilt thou say when he shall punish thee . . .?" (Jer. 13:20-21). This is a serious matter—taking care of the new converts. It is the evangelist's task to draw in the net. It is the church's task to nourish and keep them.

And yet the evangelist to some extent must also share responsibility. As a speaker he must be more than a teller of anecdotes. His sermons must be infused with the Word of God. As Paul writing to Timothy said, "Preach the word." Men's emotions must be moved, but more than that their consciences must be reached and that can only be done by probing with the Word of God. Men must know that they are lost sinners. They cannot come to God as if they were doing Him a personal favor. It has been said that "the curse of modern evangelism is in its shallowness." That was not John the Baptist's fault. He told the people to "flee from the wrath to come." And yet the preaching must be mixed with grace. A message of just "hell-fire and brimstone" without grace, often drives people further away from the Gospel.

Just joining the church is not enough. A sinner needs a new heart, and this only comes through repentance. When repentance has done its full work, converts will not be easily enticed back into the beggarly elements of the world.

The soul's greatest moment is meeting Christ. It is not a time to be hurried. It is a crime, when a soul comes forward under the burden of sin, not to be given time to meet God. The emotional outflowing of a penitent should be given full scope. When the soul hangs between life and death, the matter of wrong instruction may have the most serious consequences.

When a soul has repented, then comes the moment it must reach out in faith. One should not ask the person, "Do you feel any better?" or "Do you think you are saved?"

The personal worker should ask him if he has accepted Christ.

The moment faith is exercised is the moment peace comes to a troubled heart and he brightens up. There must be that act of faith before the Spirit of God works the miracle in his life.

If possible it is good to have the person give a brief confession of faith. "If thou shalt confess with thy mouth the Lord Jesus, and shalt believe in thine heart that God hath raised him from the dead, thou shalt be saved" (Rom. 10:9). After this his name and address may be taken. If appropriate literature and a New Testament are available, they should be given to the new convert.

May we repeat that it is the hurried and superficial dealing with the inquirers that often is the reason why results are not up to what was expected. Thorough and conscientious work must be done by both evangelist and pastor if the results are to be lasting. Both share this responsibility.

However, once the evangelist leaves he can do no more than pray for the converts. The pastor should receive them into church membership at an early date. It is a most excellent idea to have special instruction classes for these people previous to giving them membership. They should also be baptized in water and urged to receive the Holy Spirit if they did not receive during the campaign. Young converts should be given something to do if at all possible. Perhaps there is a place in the choir or orchestra for them. Some churches assign to each convert a couple of older members who will watch over them and visit them if they are absent from the services. A special Bible study for babes in Christ is helpful. The fact that some churches manage to retain nearly all their converts is proof that it is not necessary to lose the fruits of a revival.

Now a word about evangelism in connection with divine healing. There is no doubt that the healing ministry is a powerful means to reach the unsaved. The writer has been associated in many campaigns in which healing played an important role. For one thing healing brought out the people. In many cases we started with an audience of a few hundred, and before the campaign was over the number reached into the thousands. The altar calls were inspiring. Hundreds of people who never came to an altar before signified their desire to accept Christ. When they saw miracles occurring before their eyes their faith was wonderfully strengthened.

Nevertheless, much planning is needed in these types of meetings. Teaching services either in the morning or afternoon are essential. People need to know how to keep their healing after they are delivered. Sinners need to be instructed to accept Christ as their Saviour before they ask Him to heal them. Trained workers should be on hand to deal with each inquirer. Churches should recognize their opportunity. Some congregations go through many months without a single convert. Yet in meetings of this nature the opportunity to gather in a large harvest is present if the church is ready to take advantage of it.

It is important that an evangelist should have an understanding with the pastor in the matter of finances. If there is no such understanding, then the evangelist must be satisfied with whatever he receives. He must remember that he is a guest in that church.

Sometimes an evangelist goes to a church where there is a large congregation. He has expectations of a liberal offering, but in this he may be disappointed. In fact his offering may be less than that which he received in a much smaller church. He cannot understand why this should be. Such a situation sometimes results in "bad blood" between him and the pastor, with injury to the reputations of both.

There are of course many reasons why things like this happen. The pastor, or a previous pastor, may have sunk the church in debt trying to build an impressive place of worship. Of course a congregation should have as nice a church as they can properly afford. But there may have been more enthusiasm displayed in the effort than faith. The result is that the congregation is saddled with a debt that puts it under a severe financial strain. An evangelist coming into such a situation may well receive less than he anticipates. He is preaching in a beautiful church, but it may be struggling under an almost unbearable debt.

The evangelist in turn may use unfair methods in his dealings with his pastor. We have heard of cases in which the evangelist asked permission to take up a missionary offering during the campaign and got the pastor to agree. But what the pastor did not know was that the evangelist had plans to pledge up the people to large sums of money, involving thousands of dollars. When that happened the pastor was surprised and angered. It is not unlikely that after such an experience he sent out word to beware of this man.

The evangelist who intends to take up a missionary offering should explain beforehand exactly all that is involved. If the pastor then agrees, there can be no reason for him to complain. He may actually be interested in the evangelist's missionary program. He wants to be certain however that the money will go for the purpose for which it is taken. However, as can be understood, the pastor could not allow many such appeals in his church. At all events it is very wrong to take the pastor by surprise.

Unless an agreement is reached by which the evangelist is allowed to take up special offerings, he should if he intends to develop a missionary program of considerable scope, plan his campaigns outside the churches. If he finds he is not successful in this he must be content to hold his meetings in churches and conform to the pastor's wishes. An evangelist can have his ministry suffer seriously by tactics that arouse a pastor's hostility. He should remember that the shepherd of the flock has a church board to account to, and the minister can endanger his own position by allowing such things to happen.

It may seem unfortunate that such matters as money have to be discussed when souls are at stake. Still it is usual for the pastor to have an understanding with the church about his salary, and if so, then it should be no more than fair that the evangelist should also have the same. At any rate an understanding beforehand is better than a misunderstanding afterwards.

To be frank, unless an evangelist has a ministry which reaches people on a large scale, it is wise on his part that he does not involve himself in obligations of such a nature that will place himself in a compromising position with his creditors. A prayerful ministry will make a stronger impression on a congregation than possession of a luxury car and luxury equipment which may involve him in a heavy debt. An evangelist should remember that he must be subject to the generosity of the church (or the lack of it), which is host to him. He cannot afford to have a misunderstanding that will result in ill reports circulating about him. The truth is, the average young minister fares far better than the previous generation of evangelists who pioneered the message of Pentecost. Certainly he who preaches from church to church must learn to live within his means. Part of his reward must be the joy of being a reaper of souls where others have sowed in tears.

On the other hand, a church which involves itself in obligations of such a nature that it is forced to be niggardly with its speakers will suffer in the long run. God's law of giving is ever true—those who give sparingly shall reap sparingly. The pastor who becomes known as a man who plays ill with his evangelists may in time find himself rejected by both his congregation and other ministers.

Since a considerable number of young preachers serve for a time as evangelists, their attitude and method of handling finances may materially determine the course that their ministry will take. Generally speaking, ministers must have a good report if they are to achieve success. It is not enough to have it said that a man is a good preacher, but the question is, does he play the game fair in his dealings with others? If this question cannot be answered in the affirmative, then that minister may be on his way to serious trouble, no matter how outstanding he is as a preacher.

So far we have not mentioned the faith element in relation to finances. The man who takes the position of faith in his dependence on God will find that He will provide for his daily needs. Our God is a God of miracles. He that looks to God will find that He overrules the failings and frailties of men. The Lord who took five loaves and a few small fishes and broke them to feed the multitude is able to bless what seems little and multiply it until all needs are met. He who told Peter to go out and find a coin in the fish's mouth will surely answer the faith of the man who puts his trust in Him.

CHAPTER 14

Are There Apostles Today?

"And he gave some, apostles; and some, prophets; and some, evangelists; and some, pastors and teachers; For the perfecting of the saints, for the work of the ministry, for the edifying of the body of Christ: Till we all come in the unity of the faith, and of the knowledge of the Son of God, unto a perfect man, unto the measure of the stature of the fulness of Christ: That we henceforth be no more children, tossed to and fro, and carried about with every wind of doctrine, by the sleight of men, and cunning craftiness, whereby they lie in wait to deceive" (Ephes. 4:11-14).

The word "apostle" has a much wider meaning than is generally understood. The word comes from "apostolos" which means "one sent forth, a messenger, an ambassador." An apostle is one that is sent on a special mission.

The Scriptures show that there are different orders of apostles. Thus Christ Himself is spoken of as an apostle. "Wherefore holy brethren, partakers of the heavenly calling, consider the Apostle and High Priest of our profession, Christ Jesus" (Heb. 3:1). Christ was sent to this world by the Father on a mission of redemption. As the "Sent One" He was an apostle.

Then there are the Twelve Apostles of the Lamb. These were given a distinctive mission, and they received exclusive promises concerning position and authority during the Millennium, that were given to no other group. The original Twelve were witnesses of the resurrection and ascension of the Lord (Acts 1:21-22). In the choosing of Matthias, Peter stood up and said: "Beginning from the baptism of John unto the same day that he was taken up from us must one be ordained to be a witness with us of his resurrection" (Acts 1:22). The Twelve Apostles were given a special promise as to their position in the Kingdom at the time of the gathering of Israel. "And Jesus said unto them, Verily I say unto you, That ye which have followed me, in the regeneration, when the Son of Man shall sit on the throne of his glory, ye also shall sit upon twelve thrones, judging the twelve tribes of Israel" (Matt. 19:28).

There are those who claim that the Apostles' choice of Matthias as the apostle to take the place of Judas was not accepted by the Lord, and that Paul was chosen to fill that position. But Paul, when describing the resurrection of the Lord, declared that Christ was seen of the "Twelve" not of the "Eleven." Judas, having committed suicide, was not present; hence Matthias must have been the one indicated (I Cor. 15:5). As for Paul, he does not include himself in the Twelve, and of course could not, for he was not yet converted. Instead he declares of Christ in His post-resurrection manifestations that He appeared to him as one born out of due time. "And last of all he was seen of me also, as one born out of due time" (I Cor. 15:8).

A THIRD GROUP OF APOSTLES

Since Paul was not of the Twelve, though called an apostle, it is evident that there was yet another group of apostles. Matthias became the thirteenth because Judas had betrayed the Lord and committed suicide. He was the last of the original Twelve.

The fourteenth apostle was not Paul in order of time. It was James, the Lord's brother. Paul, speaking of his visit to Jerusalem, declares that he met James, the brother of the Lord, who was an apostle. "But other of the apostles saw I none, save James the Lord's brother" (Gal. 1:19). There were two James in the apostolic group, but neither of them was the son of a Mary. Hence this James was another apostle—the brother of the Lord. During the Lord's earthly ministry he did not believe the Lord's claims. After the resurrection of Christ he became a believer and was present at Pentecost (Acts 1:14).

The fifteenth and sixteenth apostles were Paul and Barnabas. Their office as apostles is spoken of in Acts 14:14: "Which when the apostles, Barnabas and Paul heard of, they rent their clothes, and ran in among the people, crying out, And saying Sirs, why do you these things?"

Paul calls Apollos an apostle. In I Corinthians 4:6-9 he says, "These things, brethren, I have in a figure transferred to myself and Apollos for your sakes." And then in verse nine, "For I think that God hath set forth us the apostles," evidently linking Apollos with himself as an apostle. Thus Apollos is the seventeenth apostle.

In the sixteenth chapter of Romans we have a remarkable declaration by Paul concerning Andronicus and Junia. In the seventh verse he says, "Salute Andronicus and Junia, my kinsmen and fellow-prisoners, and who are of note among the apostles, who were also in Christ before me." Here the apostle declares that Junia and Andronicus were older than he in the Lord, were fellow-prisoners, and were of note among the apostles. As one writer puts it, "If we were to say that a certain man was of note among the ministers, would we mean anything else but that he was a minister?" The meaning is clear that Andronicus and Junia were the eighteenth and nineteenth apostles.

In Philippians 2:25 the apostle Paul speaks of Epaphroditus as his brother and companion in the Lord. He also speaks of him as "your messenger." But this word in the original Greek is "apostolos" or apostle. Thus Epaphroditus is the twentieth of the apostles mentioned in the Scriptures.

So we see that there were other apostles besides the original Twelve. Evidently the office of apostle was to continue in the church. But here we need a word of caution. Since the office of apostle is of such importance in the church, it is certain that Satan would seek to imitate it and raise up counterfeit apostles.

Only God can set apostles in the church. He who usurps this position is a false apostle. Some who attempted to do this in the Early Church were denounced (II Cor. 11:13-15). False apostles are identified by their failure to produce the works of an apostle. In the Early Church such were tried and exposed.

It is evident that the office of an apostle is needed in the church today. *But history shows the danger of any man calling himself by this title.* Groups that have attempted to restore apostolic functions by electing apostles have merely exposed their own folly.

True apostles will manifest their calling, first by humility and a willingness to serve the body of Christ rather than by a public proclamation of their office. One can do the work of an apostle without calling himself an apostle. Actually the office is to a great extent misunderstood. Many think that it is an elevation to a position of authority whereby they may rule over God's people. The words of Jesus show how wrong such a conception is:

> "But Jesus called them unto him, and said, Ye know that the princes of the Gentiles exercise dominion over them, and they that are great exercise authority upon them. But it shall not be so among you: but who soever will be great among

you, let him be your minister; And whosoever will be chief among you, let him be your servant: Even as the Son of man came not to be ministered unto, but to minister, and to give his life a ransom for many" (Matt. 20:25-28).

Let one do the works of an apostle, and he will find that his ministry will become recognized.

There are other marks of an apostle. He will not manifest a covetous spirit for filthy lucre as did Judas. He will be a faithful steward and will not lavish on himself money given to the cause of Christ for the work of the kingdom.

True apostles will seek the unity of the body of Christ and will not try to divide it to further personal ambition nor to seek the glory of men (John 5:44; III John 9).

An apostle possesses a supernatural ministry. For his work he must be armed with special gifts of the Spirit. Thus it was in the Early Church.

"And with great power gave the apostles witness of the resurrection of the Lord Jesus: and great grace was upon them all . . . And by the hands of the apostles were many signs and wonders wrought among the people . . ." (Acts 4:33; 5:12).

In writing to the Corinthians Paul says, "Truly the signs of an apostle were wrought among you in all patience, in signs, and wonders, and mighty deeds" (II Cor. 12:12). But even signs and wonders are not sufficient to qualify one as an apostle. Evangelists, prophets, and even deacons possessed such a ministry in the Early Church. The apostle must have other qualifications.

Apostles minister discipline supernaturally. It is a mark of an apostle that when the exercise of severe discipline is needed in the church, he will administer it supernaturally. The methods used by the apostles kept the church of their day pure and free of evil elements (I Cor. 5:1-5; I Tim. 1:19-20; II Tim. 2:16-18).

The apostle is a messenger; he is sent on a mission. The vision of his soul is to see the world evangelized for Christ, to fulfill the Great Commission that Christ gave (Mark 16:15; Matt. 24:14).

An apostle will be a man of sound words. Since his work is to bring men into a knowledge of the Son of God so that they will "be no more children, tossed to and fro by every wind of doctrine," he will be a man of sound faith and purity of doctrine. The great apostle Paul in writing to Timothy and Titus exhorted them repeatedly to hold sound doctrine and to avoid those things that excite curiosity and vain arguing, which do not edify the church.

As a last word on this subject, we believe that we cannot do better than quote from Lewi Pethrus' book *The Wind Bloweth Where it Listeth*:

"Some have found fault with us because we have not been anxious to choose or elect apostles. Church history reveals that at certain periods such acts and steps have been taken. When some strong and mighty spiritual movement has broken loose, many have suggested that we might choose twelve apostles. The Irvingians chose twelve apostles, and they held forth that Jesus would come before they died. The last apostle died twenty years ago. Because we have not given ourselves to such practices, some have said that we do not respect the office of an apostle. We believe in the ministration of an apostle's office, just as much as in the pastor's or teacher's ministrations. This must continue in the Christian church.

"For my part, I have always had a sense of fear concerning these high ministrations. I have felt that much that concerns them might be misinterpreted and misunderstood. There are those who go about calling themselves apostles. A few months ago I noticed something that brought me deliverance on this point. I was reading about John the Baptist. Jesus more than once said that John the Baptist was that Elijah that should come. He said it as he preached to the people, and also as He came from the Mount of Transfiguration. The disciples understood Him. Then they went to John personally and asked him, 'Are you the Elijah that is to come?' And he answered, 'No.' Then they said, 'Who are you?' He said, 'I am the voice of one crying in the wilderness.' This enlightened me. I learned that one may have a high calling and ministration without knowing it. John did not consider himself that Elijah. Jesus did. Then, too, I learned that we need not go about trumpeting our calling and attracting attention to ourselves.

"It is impossible for humans to choose those who are to be given spiritual ministrations. Delegates of a church or denomination can never know what God may deposit in an individual's life. Organs and members of a body are not placed there mechanically. They come through a process of life. For instance, take a character like Martin Luther. No human chose him to be a reformer. He arose nevertheless. Popes decreed that he should not live, but he lived. Those that God sends are equipped and bring forth a wonderful service. 'But now hath God set the members every one of them in the body, as it hath pleased him' (1 Cor. 12:18). These administrations cannot be set in the church through the choice of majorities. God alone does this work. Ephesians 4:11 tells us, 'He (God) gave some, apostles; and some, prophets; and some, evangelists;

and some, pastors and teachers.' These are God's gifts to the church. Those having such a spiritual ministry have received it from God directly. He has deposited within them His power and they cannot be set aside by humans. Who could set aside a Luther or a Wesley? Such gifts to the church come and go without anyone's appointing them or dismissing them."

THE MINISTRY OF A PROPHET

While we are on this subject we will say a few words concerning a prophet's ministry. This ministry is an integral part of the New Testament Church and is second in importance and order in the body of Christ. There were for example at least three prophets in the Corinthian Church (I Cor. 14:29).

A prophet possesses first of all a definite gift of prophecy, usually revelatory in nature, in addition to exhortational prophecy. A true prophet will show humility and will be amenable to advice from other ministry-gifts set in the church. "If any man think himself to be a prophet, or spiritual, let him acknowledge that the things that I write unto you are the commandments of the Lord" (I Cor. 14:37). We recall the case of one man who clearly had the ministry of a prophet, but when he reached the point of considering himself infallible, his downfall was not far away.

Although the gift of prophecy is infallible when the prophet is perfectly yielded to the Spirit, New Testament prophets were not considered infallible. "Let the prophets speak two or three and let the other judge" (I Cor. 14:29). It is quite proper to judge all prophecy in the light of the Scriptures.

Included in the ministry of the prophet is an ability on occasion to foresee events of the future. Agabus warned the church of an approaching dearth. Forewarned, the church at Antioch was able to send relief in good time to the brethren in Judea (Acts 11:27,30).

Prophets are a part of the foundation of the New Testament Church. Nevertheless, the apostle John sounded a word of warning against false prophets (I John 4:1). Jesus said, "By their fruits ye shall know them"—not altogether by their gifts (Matt. 7:20-22). True prophets will have the Spirit of Christ. On the other hand, false prophets are known by their nature. Though wearing sheep's clothing, they may be cruel and relentless when crossed. They may camouflage their exterior, but sooner or later their true character will be revealed.

CHAPTER 15

The Secret of Evangelizing
A Community

A young minister's first church is usually a small one, or he may build one from the ground up. Almost all large churches have had small congregations to begin with. Certainly the pastor doubly appreciates those who help him in the early years of his ministry. Nevertheless, no pastor if he has any vision at all wishes to spend his years with only a handful of people. So hopefully he puts forth efforts to enlarge his congregation. He may secure the services of evangelists several times a year. He may give prizes to those who bring the most new people to church. He may even devote much time to prayer. And here indeed he is on the right track—*church growth is of little value unless it is backed up with prayer.* Nonetheless, some churches, despite all efforts seem to remain small. Although the pastor may appear outwardly cheerful, inwardly he is disturbed. He does not know exactly why it should be this way, but he knows that somehow he has failed.

Moreover, because his people are few in number, his income is limited. It may be that his wife has to work. He is not able to provide for his family as he would like. The facilities of his church may be inadequate because of the lack of funds, but he sees no way to enlarge nor to improve them. He labors diligently to prepare his sermons for Sunday, but there are few outsiders to benefit from his efforts. Occasionally a new family moves into the neighborhood and begins attending, and this is encouraging. But then others move out. The pastor feels he is caught in a web of circumstances from which he cannot extricate himself.

What is the answer to his problem? There is an answer! Although many churches have prayed for years for a "breakthrough" and have never gotten it, the difficulty usually lies in the fact that after they prayed they never "put legs" to their prayers! They never went out after the sinner. Yet that is what Christ and the disciples did. Businesses grow because the people go out after their clients. But too often the minister and his congregation wait for the people to come to them. Truly the words of Jesus are applicable here: "The children of this world are wiser in their generation than the children of light." They are wiser in the way they conduct their business than many Christians.

We are here speaking of the ministry of visitation as a means by which a small congregation can become a large one. By all means let the church continue praying; but let the minister and his congregation initiate a methodical plan of visitation and personal witnessing to the people of their community. We may add that this ministry of visitation is not only for the small church but also for the large one. A certain church in Dallas has one of the largest, if not the largest Protestant memberships in the world. But the congregation does not rest on its laurels, but carries on an active visitation program the year around.

What is the art of visitation? How can it be initiated? Naturally in a volume of this size we cannot go into the subject in detail. Nevertheless, we shall in brief give the Bible basis for this ministry of church evangelism.

THE ART OF VISITATION

Just before Jesus departed this world, He gave to His disciples the Great Commission. He said, "Go ye into all the world, and preach the gospel to every creature. He that believeth and is baptized shall be saved; but he that believeth not shall be damned" (Mark 16:15,16). Christ's plan for world evangelism was simple. It was nothing more than winning the person next to Him. Then he wins the one next to him, and so on until the whole world is reached.

The initial emphasis was not on missionary work in foreign lands, although that was included, but the work was to begin at home in Jerusalem and then expand in ever-widening circles until the nations of the world were reached. In other words, the carrying out of the Great Commission involves the winning of the men and women in one's neighborhood as much as winning the soul in the heathen land. Most of us can never go to a distant land; therefore, our first responsibility is to those of our own community.

The ministry of visitation was foreshadowed in God's relation with the first members of the human family. The Lord visited Adam and Eve in the Garden of Eden. He visited the children of Israel in the day of the Exodus. Christ's incarnation was God visiting His people in the veil of the flesh (Luke 1:68). When the Lord began His ministry, He visited the people in their homes. His first miracle was performed in a home (John 2). He was often found in the dwellings of publicans and sinners. Likewise He sent His disciples into the homes of the people saying, "And into whatsoever house ye enter, first say, Peace be to this house" (Luke 10:5).

Christ accomplished much of His work through personal testimony. He often avoided the multitudes that He might speak to a single person. An example is His visit with the woman at the well. She was a sinful woman, and her problem was of a nature that was best dealt with in private.

When Jesus came to Jericho, He chose to stay in the home of Zaccheus, the tax-gatherer, a profession notorious for its dishonesty. Although the gospels give only brief sketches of Christ's life, we see that visiting in the homes was one of the most important aspects of His ministry. Christ's calls were never mere social visits, but He used the time to impart spiritual instruction.

It is clear that Jesus did not depend altogether on His public preaching nor His miracles alone to accomplish His mission, but His work to a large extent was carried on through the teaching of individuals and small groups, who in time would be able to teach others. As a matter of fact, the ministry of visitation in homes was a method generally used in the Early Church. We are told that the first converts followed the apostles' example in prayers and "breaking of bread" from house to house (Acts 2:42-46; 5:42). The apostle Paul, the most tireless of the apostles, when bidding farewell to the church at Ephesus, called their attention to the fact that he had been faithful in teaching the people publicly and "from house to house."

> "And when they were come to him, he said unto them, Ye know, from the first day that I came into Asia, after what manner I have been with you at all seasons, Serving the Lord with all humility of mind, and with many tears, and temptations, which befell me by the lying in wait of the Jews: And how I kept back nothing that was profitable unto you, but have shewed you, and have taught you publicly, and from house to house" (Acts 20:18-21).

Church history tells us that the spread of the gospel in the early centuries, despite intense persecution, was extremely rapid. This tremendous growth was largely the result of their visitation program. When persecution scattered the church at Jerusalem the individual members did not relax for a moment, but they went everywhere preaching the word (Acts 8:4). Each Christian became a firebrand carrying the gospel wherever he went. Evangelization in those days was not accomplished by means of great cathedrals, robed choirs, pipe organs, educational buildings—valuable as these may be. It came largely as a result of personal work. Churches that are small and have little equipment can take heart. If they have the holy fire in their souls, they can build a strong congregation through personal work and house to house visitation.

John T. Sisamore in his excellent book *The Ministry of Visitation* makes this thoughtful comment:

> "Two thousand years have come and gone since Jesus left His command to disciple the world. Yet there are multiplied thousands who have never heard the gospel story. What is wrong? Is the plan of God inadequate for the task? Is it too idealistic? The fault does not lie in God's plan of work. The actual difficulty is that the plan has not been properly used by many churches.
>
> "Although much progress has been made in recent years in returning to God's plan for reaching people, there is still much to be done. It is true that visitation has always characterized successful churches. Nevertheless, many churches today are making little progress in their community largely because they have no practical plan for getting into the homes of people. Others have depended on Christian fellowship as a substitute for visitation, forgetting that filling church buildings is contingent upon going out after the people."

It is not enough, however, to tell people that they ought to be soul winners or that a church should conduct a visitation program. Conceding that the training of a workman and the lack of training in another is often the difference between success and failure, the question is, how does one go about organizing a program of visitation?

Effective visitation must be vigorously promoted. To reach the multitudes of the unchurched requires continuous effort. A plan that operates only for a few weeks will not accomplish much. It must become as regular a part of the church program as the prayer meeting or the morning worship hour. It must be kept continually before the congregation.

Visitation to be effective must be systematic. In a well-organized program, the workers meet weekly at the church where they receive their assignments and special instructions. After the visits are made, the workers return to the church for refreshments and a time of sharing experiences. While the enthusiasm of their new contacts is still fresh, they can share with one another what the Lord has accomplished through their efforts. "The seventy returned again with joy" to give their report (Luke 10:17).

In a special canvass, one or two full weeks may be given wholly to this program.

A master card file of prospects should be maintained where pertinent information regarding the results of each visit can be recorded on the prospect's card. Each card should also show the prospect's name, address, approximate age, sex, the ages of the other members in the family (and if they are prospects), whether the person has a church home, and whether he is a prospect for further visits. Unchurched people are priority prospects.

Sunday school absentees will, of course, be contacted by the teachers of each individual class. A personal visit by the teacher or by one whom the pastor appoints is the best type of contact. However, if this is not possible, a phone call should be made or a card should be mailed to show that the presence of each member is vital to the success of the class, and that each one is missed when he is not there. Consistent follow-up of absentees will pay rich dividends in Sunday school growth.

Although the pastor must organize and oversee the work, it is well if possible to select a layman to superintend the visitation in the same way that a Sunday school program requires a person with special qualifications. That he should be born again goes without saying; he should also be filled with the Spirit. He should be familiar with the work of the church and be a person of unquestioned loyalty. He should be able to work well with people and inspire their cooperation to win souls.

It is important that workers be trained. Those who are inexperienced should be assigned to another worker until they have learned soul winning and visitation.

There are two ways that a visitation program can be developed. (1) When there is a large number of workers, saturation coverage of a designated area can be achieved. That is, the workers visit each home in the area. (2) A church can base its visitation on a master file of prospects, which can be built in a number of ways. Naturally, if there is an extensive file of good prospects, the results of the visitation will be proportionately greater than if the time is spent visiting every home in the community.

If a church has few prospects to visit, it might be well to begin by taking a religious census. The census should include the homes nearest the church, gradually radiating out in wider and wider circles. A special census card should be provided workers. Each person should be trained in the proper approach in order to make the best impression on the people whom they visit. At homes where the families are unattached to a church, the worker should leave an invitation to attend the services.

Visitation workers should also carry a supply of cards which can be left at those houses where no one is at home, letting the family know that they were visited by the church. Many churches use attractively designed "door-knob hangers" for this purpose.

WE PROVED IT WOULD WORK

The method described above is not a new one, but it has been neglected. It is a tried and tested means of evangelization that was employed consistently by the Early Church. It is the person-to-person method. The writer proved it in actual practice in a city of 7,000 people. Our town was a community of retired people, not the kind of place where one can easily reach new people. The church we took had had excellent pastors in the past, men with an evangelistic ministry. Yet the church did not grow. People just would not come. When we took the pastorate, it was only a small congregation. We saw at once that to depend on reaching the neighborhood solely through Sunday night evangelistic services would probably be disappointing. We resolved, therefore, to start a visitation program and go from house to house throughout the whole community if necessary, to get a breakthrough for the church.

That is what we did. Soon we had other members of the congregation enthusiastic in the program. Before long we had so many new contacts that as pastors we had to restrict our visits only to the best prospects.

As a result, in a short time we had many new people in the church. The visitation plan together with a strong evangelistic program resulted in a constant stream of new converts. The new blood in the church created a rising enthusiasm, a new faith among the people. They began to pray as they had never prayed before; they prayed in faith. The church constantly grew. Few of the new converts were lost. Attendance doubled, tripled, quadrupled and soon exceeded that of any other church in the community. (See our book, *The Art of Visitation,* for further information.)

CHAPTER 16

Christian Counseling

There is nothing new about Christian counseling. From the time that there was a pastor to the present day, counseling has always been a first among his duties. He counsels in the home, in the sick room, in the hospital, in the jail, and in his office. The minister is expected to counsel when families are about to take a new step in business, when there are difficulties in the home, when adolescents get into trouble, when young people are about to be married, etc.

In recent years, however, pastoral counseling has taken on a new meaning. It has become more specialized. For this the pastor needs training. Previously he has had to rely upon his own good sense, his accumulated store of knowledge, his personal study of the Scriptures, and experiences of everyday life.

But what took a lifetime to learn previously, now needs to be put into action as quickly as possible. We are living in a day when there are many troubled people.

Off-the-cuff advice may not meet a special need. This need for counseling has given rise to an entirely new profession called psychiatry. Whether we like it or not, the facts are that psychiatrists are beginning to make perceptible inroads into the church. They have learned how they can secure rapport with the patient, while the pastor too often is at loss as to the proper approach to help these people.

There are some Christian psychiatrists who we understand are doing good work. Unfortunately most psychiatrists do not have a personal born-again experience, and although they are able to bring relief to some, the process employed by them takes many sessions, is extremely expensive and operates largely in the psychological realm. While they may be able to relieve tensions, they cannot bring relief to the sin-burdened soul. That large numbers of prominent people, including society matrons, movie actors and actresses, professional people, executives holding responsible positions, and even psychiatrists themselves, are increasingly seeking clinical help from these professionals, points up the fact that people in general realize that they have some deep lack in their lives and are desperately seeking the answer.

More and more the pastor is being called upon for special counseling. He should, therefore, have certain preparation for this work. First, of course, a minister must have a working knowledge of the Scriptures, so that he can bring peace to the troubled soul through Christ. The trained pastor is in a far superior position to a psychiatrist to help people. He has the power of God to back up his counseling. The non-Christian psychiatrist does not know how to liberate men and women from the unseen evil powers. He himself is under bondage to habits and sins from which he cannot extricate himself. Consequently his goal is not to set the patient free from his sin-load. Instead of helping him to get release from his guilt the secular psychiatrist seeks to find a way by which the patient can learn to live with it, and as much as possible forget it. *The God-anointed man is not only able to instruct the disturbed, but he is also able to pray the prayer of faith that will deliver the victim from the evil powers which are largely responsible for his woes.*

In the course of counseling a pastor seeks to get insight into the person's inner conflicts and thus to reach the cause of his difficulty. It may be misplaced loyalties, futile ambitions, unfounded jealousies, envy of the success of others, hidden hostilities, emotions which the person may not have recognized himself. The pastor by wise counsel may help that individual to reshape his personality, so that his warped outlook is replaced by a wholesome and Christ-like attitude toward life.

The pastor at all times should direct his counseling in accordance with the Scriptures, so that the person may know that he is being guided by the Word of God and not human wisdom.

Such is the pastor's true task. How much better that he should spend his time counseling with and ministering to people than running trivial and petty errands for them or being their choreboy, although in an emergency he will quickly respond with any aid he can give. In helping people through their problems and difficulties by wise counseling, the pastor binds them closely to himself and the church.

There are some dangers in counseling that should be avoided. The pastor should budget his time. He has many other duties demanding his attention. He cannot as a psychiatrist spend long hours with patients. Nor is this necessary. When the heart of a problem is discovered, the Word of God and the prayer of faith should result in the person's deliverance.

For a pastor to counsel effectively, he must first secure the person's confidence. The troubled individual must feel that the pastor is seeing things through his eyes and is able to understand his point of view. Most important the minister must live the life before the people. When a member of the congregation says, "Pastor, I have been watching your life, and I know I can confide in you," the minister is in an excellent position to help that person.

The preacher, therefore, must study the needs of the people. He must be prepared beforehand to understand how to counsel with young people who are about to be married. He should know exactly what words to give in the hour when death strikes in a home. It is in the pastor's hand to bring peace of mind to a person when a loved one has suddenly been taken away. He should be able to comfort and help the aged with their problems.

He should be familiar with the community agencies and where expert help can be obtained when needed. He should be able to give advice concerning social agencies, schools, hospitals, etc. As the pastor serves the individual, so the person in turn learns to serve the church and to share its responsibilities. The work has immediate reward, for in his training of people for fields of service, they will relieve the pastor of routine burdens so that he can devote his time to the more important things.

And now a word in conclusion. In counseling people, the pastor must love them. He is not a professional who is retained for a fee. The relationship is much closer. The poor, as well as the rich are equally entitled to his services. He is their confidant. When people have confidence in a pastor they may on occasion confess dark secrets in their lives. The minister must hold these disclosures in strict confidence. He should withhold judgment, censure, or revulsion. He does not sit as a judge in court, but rather as an advocate who is using his abilities to advance his clients' welfare. In other words, he is leading his people away from troubled paths into a victorious walk with Christ.

In a way he must be all things to all men. Penitent sinners often find absolution when they can pour out their sins and confess their own degradation. Children feel that they are persons when the pastor listens to them. Elderly people need someone to whom they can open their hearts.

Finally may we say that after giving the person an opportunity to state his case, it is advisable for the pastor to guide the session. Once the person has unburdened his soul, it will not do to allow him to go over the same ground again and recount all the morbid details of his case. But if not guided, this is the very thing a troubled mind is likely to do. Faith does not come by dwelling on symptoms but rather upon God's promises.

Let the person confess his sins; let him open his heart and tell of his problems, but when he has done this, it is enough. He should consider the past a closed gate. Now he should look forward to broader fields, to God's promises that are his for the taking. At this moment the pastor may rise, lay his hands upon the person and pray for deliverance. The prayer of faith is an essential part of a pastor's counseling. "Whatsoever things ye desire, when ye pray, believe that ye receive" (Mark 11:24). After praying, the pastor should leave at once.

CHAPTER 17

The Doctrine of Christ—Basis
of Fellowship

What is the doctrinal basis of fellowship for those who are members of the body of Christ? Over the centuries men have set forth numerous doctrinal statements which their authors claim to be the true basis of Christian fellowship. These doctrinal statements which vary materially one from another have often served to divide rather than to unite Christians.

Actually the Bible has given us its own inspired statement of faith, although strangely enough, comparatively few people are acquainted with it or recognize its significance. Yet it is there; and for all believers of the Scriptures, it should be accepted as the doctrinal basis of fellowship of the followers of Christ. John the apostle refers to this in II John 9-11 as the *"doctrine of Christ."*

> "He that abideth in the doctrine of Christ, he hath both the Father and the Son. *If there come any unto you, and bring not this doctrine, receive him not in your house, neither bid him God speed"* (II John 9-11).

The doctrinal basis of fellowship, therefore, is belief in and practice of the principles of the doctrine of Christ. We find in Hebrews 6:1-2 a statement of these basic principles of the doctrine of Christ.

> "Therefore leaving the principles of the doctrine of Christ, let us go on unto perfection; not laying again the foundation of repentance from dead works, and of faith toward God, Of the doctrine of baptisms, and of laying on of hands, and of resurrection of the dead, and of eternal judgment."

Here we find six things and a seventh implied which comprise the principles of the doctrine of Christ. We are also informed that if one denies or forsakes them, he jeopardizes his part in the body of Christ. These seven principles are as follows: repentance from dead works; faith toward God; doctrine of baptisms; laying on of hands; resurrection of the dead; eternal judgment; the going "on to perfection."

98

Many statements of faith have been drawn up, and numerous have been the controversies over what should be included and what should be left out in such a statement. Here is an inspired list of the essentials. Controversy is excluded unless one wishes to dispute with inspiration. There are seven principles of the doctrine of Christ. One can be honestly ignorant of them, but to turn from them once they have been known is to "fall away" and become apostate.

> "For it is impossible for those who were once enlightened, and have tasted of the heavenly gift, and were made partakers of the Holy Ghost, And have tasted the good word of God, and the powers of the world to come, If they shall fall away, to renew them again unto repentance; seeing they crucify to themselves the Son of God afresh, and put him to an open shame" (Heb. 6:4-6).

The doctrine of Christ provides enlightenment, tasting of the heavenly gift, partaking of the Holy Ghost, tasting of the good word of God, and of the powers of the world to come.

Truly these represent an apostolic experience! The above experience provides the basis of apostolic fellowship. Now let us consider each of these seven great principles of the doctrine of Christ.

DOCTRINE 1 — REPENTANCE FROM DEAD WORKS

Repentance comes first in the doctrine of Christ. Belief in Christ is not sufficient without repentance. Jesus said to the religious Jews, "Except ye repent, ye shall all likewise perish" (Luke 13:3). The natural man, if he believes in salvation at all, believes in a salvation of works. But only through the "blood of Christ" is one purged "from dead works to serve the living God" (Heb. 9:14).

This great doctrine helped Martin Luther to restore the true faith to the church in the Reformation. The Medieval Church was full of dead works. It prayed to saints, fasted, mortified the body, counted beads, bought indulgences, and made pilgrimages in an effort to obtain salvation. But all was to no avail. Without repentance there is no basis of fellowship.

DOCTRINE 2 — FAITH TOWARD GOD

The next great principle of the doctrine of Christ is "faith toward God." It is faith—not in dead works—but faith toward God through Christ. The second great truth proclaimed by the Reformation was, "The just shall live by faith." Christ showed that faith in Him is faith toward God. "No man cometh unto the Father, but by me" (John 14:6). No doctrine in the Bible is more important than the doctrine of faith in the Lord Jesus Christ. "For God so loved the world, that he gave his only begotten Son, that whosoever believeth in him should not perish, but have everlasting life" (John 3:16). "The Father loveth the Son, and hath given all things into his hand. He that believeth on the Son hath everlasting life: and he that believeth not the Son shall not see life; but the wrath of God abideth on him" (John 3:35-36). We need not elaborate on this all-important truth.

DOCTRINE 3—THE DOCTRINE OF BAPTISMS

A. WATER BAPTISM

Notice that the third principle is not the doctrine of baptism, but the doctrine of baptisms. Some believe in baptism, but not in baptisms.

Water baptism is the first baptism. Jesus showed this was his doctrine by saying, "He that believeth and is baptized shall be saved." Peter explained that water baptism is a figure, or symbol, of an inward work—"the answer of a good conscience."

> "The like figure whereunto even baptism doth also now save us (not the putting away of the filth of the flesh, but the answer of a good conscience toward God,) by the resurrection of Jesus Christ" (I Peter 3:21).

The answer of a good conscience saves us. Paul specifically shows that *controversy over baptism* does not save us.

> "Is Christ divided? was Paul crucified for you? or were ye baptized in the name of Paul? I thank God that I baptized none of you, but Crispus and Gaius; Lest any should say that I had baptized in mine own name. And I baptized also the household of Stephanas: besides, I know not whether I baptized any other. For Christ sent me not to baptize, but to preach the gospel: not with wisdom of words, lest the cross of Christ should be made of none effect" (I Cor. 1:13-17).

Baptism is the answer of a good conscience before God. It is an outward symbol of initiation into the body of Christ. Paul forbade that the rite of baptism be used to divide the body of Christ and thus defeat its own purpose. He refused to baptize in Corinth lest his act become a means of dividing the church. The matter was left to local ministers. The doctrine of Christ declares, "He that believeth and is baptized shall be saved; but he that believeth not shall be damned" (Mark 16:16).

B. BAPTISM WITH THE HOLY GHOST

Besides baptism in water, there is baptism with the Holy Ghost. This is the doctrine of Christ who said, "For John truly baptized with water; but ye shall be baptized with the Holy Ghost not many days hence" (Acts 1:5). This was the experience that the 120 received on the day of Pentecost. Peter said it "is unto you, and to your children, and to all that are afar off, even as many as the Lord our God shall call" (Acts 2:39).

Jesus at the same time that He spoke to them of the coming experience at Pentecost also revealed its great purpose—power to evangelize the world.

> "But ye shall receive power, after that the Holy Ghost is come upon you: and ye shall be witnesses unto me both in Jerusalem, and in all Judea, and in Samaria, and unto the uttermost part of the earth" (Acts 1:8).

The doctrine of the baptism in the Holy Ghost is a basic principle of the doctrine of Christ. John the Baptist spoke of Christ's baptizing His people in the Holy Ghost (Matt. 3:11-12). Those who rejected Christ were the chaff to be burned in an unquenchable fire.

C. BAPTISM INTO ONE BODY

Associated with the baptism of the Holy Ghost is the act in which the Holy Ghost Himself baptizes the members of Christ into one body. Men may join a human organization, but they become members of the body of Christ by baptism by the Spirit into the body. "For by one Spirit are we all baptized into one body" (I Cor. 12:13).

The Spirit of God has set Christ as head of the body, and all true believers are members of the body. The doctrine of baptisms thus compels us to accept and recognize the unity of all true believers.

Since the Spirit sets members in the body, no human personalities may overrule or break that relationship without violating the integrity of the body of Christ.

Who are members that are baptized by the Holy Ghost into one body? They are listed in I Corinthians 12:27-28.

101

"Now ye are the body of Christ, and members in particular. And God hath set some in the church, first apostles, secondarily prophets, thirdly teachers, after that miracles, then gifts of healings, helps, governments, diversities of tongues."

These members of the body of Christ are empowered for service by certain gifts which are given them by the Holy Ghost.

"For, to, one is given by the Spirit the word of, wisdom; to another the word of knowledge by the same Spirit; To another faith by the same Spirit; to another the gifts of healing by the same Spirit; To another the working of miracles; to another prophecy; to another discerning of spirits; to another divers kinds of tongues; to another the interpretation of tongues" (I Cor. 12:8-10).

The recognition of the gifts of the Spirit and the ministry-gifts God has given to the church is essentially the doctrine of Christ, for the Holy Ghost through baptism sets these members into the church. (Note: The theological order of these three baptisms is not necessarily the order we have used.)

THE LORD'S SUPPER

As water baptism is the outward symbol of being baptized into Christ (Romans 6:3), so the partaking of the bread in the Lord's Supper is the symbol of Christ's dwelling within us and we in Him (John 6:56). We become members of the body of Christ as we partake of Christ in faith.

"The bread which we break, is it not the communion of the body of Christ? For we being many are one bread, and one body: for we are all partakers of that one bread" (I Cor. 10:16-17).

This eating of the body of Christ and thus becoming a part of His body is one of the great doctrines of Christ. The Lord repeated the truth over and over in His sermon in John 6:53-56.

"Then Jesus said unto them, Verily, verily, I say unto you, Except ye eat the flesh of the Son of man, and drink his blood, ye have no life in you. Whoso eateth my flesh, and drinketh my blood, hath eternal life; and I will raise him up at the last day. For my flesh is meat indeed, and my blood is drink indeed. He that eateth my flesh, and drinketh my blood, dwelleth in me, and I in him."

Those who partake of Christ in faith dwell in Christ and are

102

a part of His body. This doctrine of Christ is absolutely essential for fellowship. Many who had followed the Lord until this time could not accept this doctrine. When they heard it, they turned back and walked with him no more (John 6:66).

DOCTRINE 4—THE LAYING ON OF HANDS

The next basic principle of the doctrine of Christ is the laying on of hands. This has been practiced by the church for a long time, but too often without faith and the anointing of God. In such a case it is only a form and a ceremony.

The laying on of hands was a doctrine of the Old Testament. Joshua received the spirit of wisdom through the laying on of hands by Moses, who had been so authorized by the Lord (Num. 27:18, 23; Deut. 34:9).

A. THE LAYING ON OF HANDS FOR HEALING

Jesus began His ministry of healing by laying hands on the sick. "And he could there do no mighty work, save that he laid his hands upon a few sick folk, and healed them" (Mark 6:5).

In the Great Commission, Christ mentions the laying on of hands. He commanded His disciples to lay hands on the sick for their recovery. "They shall lay hands on the sick, and they shall recover" (Mark 16:18). The apostles obeyed this command in their ministry to the sick in the Early Church. "And by the hands of the apostles were many signs and wonders wrought among the people" (Acts 5:12). Paul received his sight through the laying on of the hands of Ananias (Acts 9:17-18).

B. THE LAYING ON OF HANDS FOR THE RECEIVING OF THE HOLY SPIRIT

With the exception of the two initial spontaneous outpourings, the Holy Ghost was received by the laying on of hands. In Samaria believers received the Holy Ghost through the laying on of hands of Peter and John:

> "Now when the apostles which were at Jerusalem heard that Samaria had received the word of God, they sent unto them Peter and John: Who, when they were come down, prayed for them, that they might receive the Holy Ghost: (For as yet he was fallen upon none of them: only they that were baptized in the name of the Lord Jesus.) Then they laid their hands on them, and they received the Holy Ghost" (Acts 8:14-17).

The disciples at Ephesus received the Holy Ghost through the laying on of Paul's hands.

> ". . . Paul having passed through the upper coasts came to Ephesus: and finding certain disciples . . . And when Paul had laid his hands upon them the Holy Ghost came on them; and they spake with tongues, and prophesied" (Acts 19:1,6).

The apostle Paul himself received the Holy Ghost through the laying on of hands of Ananias, an obscure disciple (Acts 9:17). This act shows that this ministry was not reserved exclusively for the apostles.

C. LAYING ON OF HANDS FOR MINISTRY-GIFTS

There is also the laying on of hands for the several ministries. In the case of Paul and Barnabas after they had waited on the Lord with prayer and fasting, the Holy Ghost separated them for a certain work. Hands were laid upon them, and they were sent out on their mission.

> "As they ministered to the Lord, and fasted, the Holy Ghost said, Separate me Barnabas and Saul for the work whereunto I have called them. And when they had fasted and prayed, and laid hands on them, they sent them away" (Acts 13:2-3).

A gift was given to Timothy through the laying on of hands.

> "Neglect not the gift that is in thee, which was given thee by prophecy, with the laying on of the hands of the presbytery" (I Tim. 4:14).
> "Wherefore I put thee in remembrance that thou stir up the gift of God, which is in thee by the putting on of my hands" (II Tim. 1:6).

We see that in the case of Timothy that the gift was ministered to him at the time of laying on of hands and was accompanied by prophecy. Later Paul admonished Timothy to stir up the gift which had been given to him at that time.

It is evident that the laying on of hands is a cooperating with God. The Scriptures do not teach an indiscriminate laying on of hands. Paul cautioned Timothy to "lay hands suddenly on no man" (I Tim. 5:22). Timothy was a convert of Paul's and sat under his ministry. Paul knew Timothy's background and of the faith of his mother and grandmother (II Tim. 1:5). He knew these things before he laid hands on Timothy.

Only the Holy Ghost gives gifts for the ministry. It is His prerogative. "But all these worketh that one and the selfsame Spirit, dividing to every man, severally as he will" (I Cor. 12:11). The giving of the gifts belongs to God.

The initiative of stirring up the gifts belongs to man.

DOCTRINE 5—DOCTRINE OF THE RESURRECTION

The fifth essential principle of the doctrine of Christ is the doctrine of the resurrection of the dead. This glorious event takes place simultaneously with the Coming of the Lord:

> "But I would not have you to be ignorant, brethren, concerning them which are asleep, that ye sorrow not, even as others which have no hope. For if we believe that Jesus died and rose again, even so them also which sleep in Jesus will God bring with him. For this we say unto you by the word of the Lord, that we which are alive and remain unto the coming of the Lord shall not prevent them which are asleep. For the Lord himself shall descend from heaven with a shout, with the voice of the archangel, and with the trump of God: and the dead in Christ shall rise first: Then we which are alive and remain shall be caught up together with them in the clouds, to meet the Lord in the air: and so shall we ever be with the Lord" (I Thes. 4:13-17).

Jesus made it His doctrine when speaking of the resurrection of the dead in John 5:28-29.

> "Marvel not at this: for the hour is coming, in the which all that are in the graves shall hear his voice, And shall come forth; they that have done good, unto the resurrection of life; and they that have done evil, unto the resurrection of damnation."

The order of these resurrections is revealed in Revelation 20. The doctrine of the resurrection of the righteous dead and the simultaneous event, the Second Coming of Christ, is an essential principle of the doctrine of Christ. Christ spoke of this event in Matthew 24:30-31.

The glorious truth of the resurrection of all the dead was confirmed and made certain by the resurrection of Jesus Christ (I Cor. 15:12).

DOCTRINE 6—DOCTRINE OF ETERNAL JUDGMENT

This solemn truth is an essential part of the doctrine of Christ. Christ taught the reality of eternal damnation, or judgment (Mark

3:29). He referred to an everlasting fire prepared for the devil and his angels (Matt. 25:41). He spoke of everlasting punishment for the wicked (Matt. 25:46). Those who would lessen the seriousness of the truth or deny the eternalness of the judgment of God are of the same spirit as was Satan who, while in the Garden of Eden told the first lie, "Ye shall not surely die."

DOCTRINE 7—DOCTRINE OF PERFECTION

The writer of the book of Hebrews declared that these six principles of the doctrine of Christ were not complete. There was one more—Christians should "go on to perfection." They must go forward or die. Though none is already perfect, each should press toward the mark for the prize of the high calling of God in Christ Jesus (Phil. 3:12-14):

> "Not as though I had already attained, either were already perfect: but I follow after, if that I may apprehend that for which also I am apprehended of Christ Jesus. Brethren, I count not myself to have apprehended: but this one thing I do, forgetting those things which are behind, and reaching forth unto those things which are before, I press toward the mark for the prize of the high calling of God in Christ Jesus."

Not how far have we already attained, but are we pressing forward to the prize of the high calling in Christ Jesus? This is the doctrine of Christ, for He Himself said, "Be ye therefore perfect, even as your Father which is in heaven is perfect" (Matt. 5:48).

Aside from the required acceptance of the doctrine of Christ, it is evident that in the Early Church there was not uniformity of belief in many matters, as for example that of circumcision (Acts 15:1). The apostles did not attempt to resolve differences in this case. Each side was given liberty of conscience in the matter, but neither was permitted to make it an issue. The church should stand for liberty of conscience in the matter of doctrine other than the doctrine of Christ, but it must condemn and disapprove of those who would use that liberty to divide brethren.

CHAPTER 18

Divine Discipline—The Forgotten Key to Church Unity

It has often been said that unless some kind of ecclesiastical court were set up in the church on the usual lines of human government, law and order could not be maintained in the church. It is pointed out that Satan is certain to incite disorders within the church, which unless dealt with, will destroy fellowship. Some people tend to do as they please, and if there are no means of exercising discipline, how then can the unity and purity of the whole church be maintained?

In answering these questions, we are entering a field of inquiry that has been singularly avoided to the great injury of the church. It is in our adhering closely to the Scriptural method of dealing with these problems that will help us to attain the unity of the body of Christ. The divine instructions in this matter are a bold challenge of our faith. But if we have met this challenge in the same way that men of God have met other challenges, we shall succeed. The ministry of "governments" has a supernatural element in it, just the same as the gifts of healings. Those who accept the calling of the ministry of "governments" must accept the responsibility of supernaturally maintaining discipline in the church. We find this truth well illustrated in the ministry of Paul.

When Paul met a situation in Corinth in which unruly and immoral persons threatened the purity of that church, he did not tell the Corinthians that he would deal with the offenders by human methods. He said that if he came he would demonstrate the power of his authority:

> "But I will come to you shortly, if the Lord will, and will know, not the speech of them which are puffed up, but the power. For the kingdom of God is not in word, but in power. What will ye? shall I come unto you with a rod, or in love, and in the spirit of meekness?" (I Cor. 4:19-21).

Paul's words were not an idle boast. He did not propose to go to

107

Corinth to set up a human court to deal with the wicked members. Even as he wrote to the church at Corinth, the Spirit of God impressed on him to deal with one flagrant offender at once. And this he did by turning him over to Satan (I Cor. 5:3-5).

At that time the Corinthian church was not far from splitting into several factions. Some recognized Peter's authority but not Paul's (I Cor. 1:12-13). But Paul's demonstration of the power of his office had the desired effect. When the people saw his authority, the fear of God came upon them. The church in II Corinthians became a purged church and moved to a much higher spiritual life than the one in I Corinthians.

When the Scriptures speak of the essential unity of the body of Christ, it is not to be assumed that there are no qualifications that are required of those who would be members of that privileged body. The New Testament does not teach that everyone who professes to be of the body of Christ is actually a member. There are certain definite qualifications for membership. As we have already noted, there are occasions when it may be necessary for a professing member to be severed from the body. In most cases, however, discipline is to be administered to the end that the erring member may be restored.

The unity of the body of Christ depends greatly upon the proper administration of discipline according to the New Testament pattern. Otherwise, the church may find itself at the mercy of reckless persons who by their actions will deliberately disrupt or destroy that unity that their own selfish ends may be attained. The administration of discipline in the body of Christ must have a supernatural element in it just as the ministry of healing has. Supernatural discipline belongs to those whom God has appointed to "governments." God has anticipated and foreseen every means that would be employed by the devil to destroy the unity of the church and has provided an adequate method to counteract his devices. "Behold, I give unto you power to tread on serpents and scorpions, and over all the power of the enemy: and nothing shall by any means hurt you" (Luke 10:19).

Any organization requires methods of governing the body and securing the proper relationship of the members thereof. The church is an organism with the members joined together in vital relationship by the Spirit of God. The functioning of this body in the normal manner as divinely intended is spoken of in Ephesians 4:16, "From whom the whole body fitly joined together and compacted by that which every joint supplieth, according to the effectual working in the measure of every part, maketh increase of the body unto the edifying of itself in love."

Let us now note the divinely ordained method of dealing with offending brethren in the church.

FIRST STEP—GO TO ERRING BROTHER ALONE

"Moreover if thy brother shall trespass against thee, go and tell him his fault between thee and him alone: if he shall hear thee, thou hast gained thy brother" (Matt. 18:15).

This is the first step. No one has the right to complain against another member unless he has obeyed this commandment of Jesus first. Many misunderstandings disappear when brethren are willing to get together.

There may be a case in which a brother has nothing against another, but he learns that the other brother has something against him. The offending person should have taken the initiative in coming, but since he has not, the first brother should go to him:

"Therefore if thou bring thy gift to the altar, and there rememberest that thy brother hath ought against thee; Leave there thy gift before the altar, and go thy way; first be reconciled to thy brother, and then come and offer thy gift" (Matt. 5:23-24).

It is the will of God that members of the body of Christ should earnestly seek reconciliation with each other. Unfortunately, there are times when such reconciliation is difficult to obtain. The erring individual may be inclined to be stubborn in his fault.

SECOND STEP—TAKE THE ERRING BROTHER BEFORE TWO OR THREE WITNESSES

"But if he will not hear thee, then take with thee one or two more, that in the mouth of two or three witnesses every word may be established" (Matt. 18:16).

It may happen that though agreement was impossible at first, an understanding can now be found. It is possible that in the presence of other witnesses a reconciliation will be obtained.

THIRD STEP—BRING THE MATTER BEFORE THE CHURCH

"And if he shall neglect to hear them, tell it unto the church: but if he neglect to hear the church, let him be unto thee as an heathen man and a publican" (Matt. 18:17).

If the matter cannot be settled with witnesses, then it should be brought before the church. What the Scriptures tell us should follow this step reveals the shortcomings of the church in its handling of disciplinary matters.

FOURTH STEP—THE ADMINISTERING OF DISCIPLINE

The man who has been excommunicated may go quietly on his way, perhaps recognizing his wrong, though persisting in his sinful course. However, the excommunicated individual may and often does just what the devil wants him to do. He may become spiteful and use his influence to abuse those that are in the church. He may parade an injured innocence in such a way as to draw much sympathy to himself. Here is where the church too often fails. Jesus followed His instruction on excommunication with this additional statement:

> "Verily I say unto you, whatsoever ye shall bind on earth shall be bound in heaven: and whatsoever ye shall loose on earth shall be loosed in heaven" (Matt. 18:18).

What does this mean—this binding and loosing which Jesus speaks of in connection with His teaching on discipline in the church? It can mean only one thing. Law is ineffective unless there is a means by which law may be enforced. Law must have a penalty that will cause the sinner to fear to do wrong. Unless laws in the natural realm are enforced, the disobedient will make a mockery of them. Unless spiritual laws are enforced, there will be chaos in the kingdom of God on earth. The sure knowledge that penalties will be inflicted is the greatest deterrent to those who would otherwise break the laws of God.

However, the laws of the kingdom of God differ in some respects from civil law. Civil law often leaves out forgiveness and mercy and is concerned only with justice. But in the church mercy and forgiveness reign with justice. That is why the Lord in laying down the rules of church discipline gave an offending member three chances to do the right thing. All of these failing, he is at last to be dealt with. It is then that Jesus says, "Whatsoever ye shall bind on earth shall be bound in heaven: and whatsoever ye shall loose on earth shall be loosed in heaven." This verse deals with the administration of church discipline.

Let us now consider some of the cases in the New Testament in which divine discipline was administered.

THE CASE OF ANANIAS AND SAPPHIRA

Why do we have so much evil in the church? Why do professed Christians sometimes lie and steal, seemingly with impunity? The answer can only be that there is a lack of New Testament discipline.

Let us notice a case in the fifth chapter of Acts. A mighty revival was in progress in the church at Jerusalem. Its effect had been far reaching. The people in the church had only one purpose in life and that was to serve God with all their hearts. They divested themselves of their earthly possessions and had all things in common (Acts 4:32). Under the inspiration of this beautiful unselfish spirit the church prospered and the converts multiplied. Then a sinister thing happened. A certain man and his wife, Ananias and Sapphira, conspired between themselves to bring evil into the assembly. They had been swept into the church on the tide of blessing and supernatural demonstration. They had observed others who had sold their possessions and laid the money at the apostles' feet. They desired to be thought of as others, but they wanted to keep a reserve in case the enterprise fell through. So they sold a piece of land keeping back a part of the price. This was perfectly all right, except that in presenting the money to Peter they pretended that it was the whole amount. It was deliberate, premeditated hypocrisy. If they had gotten by with this deception, others would have been tempted to do the same. Soon the whole church would have been permeated with evil.

Peter by discernment of the Spirit perceived the hypocrisy. He told Ananias that the land had been his to do with as he would, but his deception was what was so wicked. In the midst of the glorious manifestation of God's power, Ananias had purposed in his heart to lie. Peter said, "Thou hast not lied unto men, but unto God" (Acts 5:3-4). Ananias upon hearing these words fell down dead at the feet of Peter. The same judgment fell upon his wife Sapphira, who came in later.

What was the result of this solemn execution of divine judgment? The consequences were that "great fear came on all them that heard these things" (Acts 5:11), and "of the rest durst no man join himself to them: but the people magnified them." That means that no more worldlings and unconverted attempted to join the church. But the truly sincere "believers were the more added to the Lord, multitudes both of men and women" (Verse 14).

111

How different might have been the result if the discipline had been attempted by carnal means. Had a church committee accused them of their act they might have denied it. Friends perhaps would have believed their story, and there would have been a rift among the people. Thus Satan would have destroyed the unity and harmony of the church. But when the discipline was administered in supernatural power, the evil was purged and a holy fear came upon the people.

DISCIPLINE FOR IMMORALITY

We have already mentioned the case of immorality in the Corinthian Church. Let us consider the matter further. It was an open case of incest, and there was no necessity of special discernment such as Peter exercised in the matter of Ananias and Sapphira. It was in fact a flagrant violation of common decency, in which a man was consorting with his father's wife! If this were allowed to go unpunished the example would have encouraged a breaking down of all restraints among the people. The Corinthian saints perhaps deplored the circumstances, but unfortunately they did nothing about it.

Paul heard about the matter. He rebuked them severely, warning them that "a little leaven leaveneth the whole lump." He implied that if the spread of evil were left unchecked, it would corrupt the whole church.

But how should this person be disciplined? Apparently the man was a self-willed individual and not easy to deal with. At any rate the Corinthian Church had been reluctant to handle the matter. If the man were confronted with his deed, he might stir up a lot of trouble. People might take sides in the matter. Certainly, immorality was a very common thing in Corinth. Paul showed them how the case was to be handled. The man was to be disciplined by supernatural means:

> "And ye are puffed up, and have not rather mourned, that he that hath done this deed might be taken away from among you. For I verily, as absent in body, but present in spirit, have judged already, as though I were present, concerning him that hath so done this deed, In the name of our Lord Jesus Christ, when you are gathered together, and my spirit, with the power of our Lord Jesus Christ, To deliver such an one unto Satan for the destruction of the flesh, that the spirit may be saved in the day of our Lord Jesus" (I Cor. 5:2-5).

Here was how the church was to administer discipline when it could not be done effectively otherwise. Christ has given the power of binding and loosing to the church. This method of divine discipline was to be used when other means did not seem advisable.

Notice, however, that the discipline administered was for the man's own good. Although Paul turned him over to Satan for the destruction of the flesh, yet it was to the end that his spirit might be saved and the man himself restored to fellowship. It was better that he suffer than be lost. As things turned out, the physical suffering that he experienced taught him that he could not trifle with the ordinances of God. We understand that the man came to the place of true repentance.

Church trials sometimes are nothing more than a laughing stock to the world. God has a way to deal with sinners in the church, which will command the respect of the culprit, of the world, and of the church. It is time we used the divine method.

Finally this method always results in true justice's being administered. Church trials sometimes terminate in a verdict of injustice. But God is a perfect judge. If a man is right in the sight of God, no man can judge him. Balaam the prophet tried to bring a curse on Israel, but his curse was turned into a blessing (Numbers 24:9-10). Only when the children of Israel sinned did the curse come upon them.

JUDGMENT OF FALSE TEACHERS

The church is sometimes faced with the problem of what to do with those who disturb the unity of the body with false doctrines and issues. Living in this imperfect age as we are, there will always be differences of opinion among the most conscientious and sincere believers. To attempt to secure conformity of belief in every detail of doctrine is impossible. The Medieval Church tried to do this by means of physical force and even torture, but it failed to accomplish its purpose. Theological controversy is not God's plan for His church.

Nevertheless, it is true that from time to time Satan inspires certain leaders with teachings that are so greatly in error that their propagation may result in serious damage to the unity of the church. What is to be done in a case like this? Should the church stand idly by and let the evil spread to the possible ruin of many souls?

The Scriptures clearly indicate that the church should do something about it. But God's way is not man's way. It is one thing to pass judgment on heresy, and it is another thing to halt its spread. Propagators of heresy, after church trials often continue to flourish, drawing many disciples after them.

However, God has a way of handling this problem. He did not omit anything that was essential to the welfare of the church. But the church often has had too little faith to employ the divine means placed at its disposal. The apostle Paul was not afraid to exercise this power. He used the binding and loosing of powers that Jesus delivered to the church.

Let us note how Paul dealt with certain ministers who had brought in teaching that was contrary to the doctrine of Christ. These leaders had denied the truth of the resurrection—that is they claimed that the resurrection was already past. This of course is a grave and dangerous error, for it violates one of the most important foundation truths of Christianity.

These men, whose names were Hymenaeus, Alexander, and Philetus (I Tim. 1:19-20, II Tim. 2:16-18) had thereby succeeded in overthrowing the faith of some. Apparently they allegorized the resurrection, as do some modernists of our day who attempt to do away with the physical resurrection. One of the men involved in the heresy, Alexander, was very bold in his opposition. He is spoken of by Paul as having "greatly withstood our words."

Paul warned Timothy against these men. Ordinarily, Paul was averse to striving over doctrinal matters, as is seen in his words in II Tim. 2:24-26.

> "And the servant of the Lord must not strive; but be gentle unto all men, apt to teach, patient, In meekness instructing those that oppose themselves; if God peradventure will give them repentance to the acknowledging of the truth; And that they may recover themselves out of the snare of the devil, who are taken captive by him at his will."

But in this case the matter was so serious that Paul felt called upon to take special measures. He, therefore, used the binding and loosing powers given the church. Paul in his epistle explained what he had done. "Of whom is Hymenaeus and Alexander; whom I have delivered unto Satan, that they may learn not to blaspheme" (I Tim. 1:20).

It is evident from these words that Paul intended that the judgment be disciplinary. He did not desire these men should lose their

114

souls. Neither did he want their perverse teachings to result in the loss of other souls. So he turned them over to Satan as he had done with the evildoer in the Corinthian church.

JUDGMENT ON OPPOSERS

The above disciplinary judgments relate to offenders within the church. There were occasions in which judgment was meted out upon religious pretenders who brazenly opposed earnest souls from turning to Christ. Such was the case in Acts 13:6-13. In this instance Elymas the sorcerer, a professed religionist who claimed to be a prophet, sought to subvert a certain deputy that had been deeply moved by the preaching of Paul. The apostle filled with the Holy Spirit turned to the sorcerer and pronounced judgment upon him (Acts 13:10-11). The man was smitten with blindness. The immediate result of this act was the conversion of the deputy.

CHAPTER 19

Why Leaders Fail

THE DANGER OF A QUICK SUCCESS

Every minister prays for success in his chosen work. Many dream of the "big break." Well and good. But if and when this happens, there is a danger that the man may become swept away by his own successes. He may dream of still bigger things, forgetting that the first step is to consolidate gains already won. He may overlook the fact that the devil is busy laying plans for the downfall of all who are used of God in a special way.

A grave danger is that on the strength of the extra finances that come in, the minister will involve himself in obligations which he may not be able to meet. When creditors press for payment and there is no immediate source of help, we have seen elation replaced by fear and even by terror. The man may be tempted to do something desperate. If he does not face the situation honestly, his actions may not only become a reproach to the cause, but they may saddle him with an image of irresponsibility that will hinder his ministry from that time on.

Some years ago I invited a young man whose ministry was showing great promise, to hold a campaign with me. He actually was being used of God in a special way and was reaching many souls for Christ. However, something happened at the close of our first meeting together, which indicated the future course of his ministry. The audience attending the meetings reached about 1500 in number, which was many more than he had ever had in his services before. Consequently his offerings were several times larger than he had previously received. After the close of the meeting I did not see him for several days. When I met him again, I found that he had made an investment—he proudly informed me that he had just put money down on a brand new Cadillac! In high spirits he went on to elaborate the great advantages of owning a Cadillac. He said that the added comfort was worth it in his evangelistic tours. He needed a fast means of transportation to take him across the country. (One fast trip across the country brought him three traffic fines.) Moreover, he added it would indicate to the people the new status of his ministry!

We are not saying that it is wrong for a minister with a large congregation who may be expected to live on the same level as they, to own a Cadillac. But it was altogether out of place for a young man who had been in the ministry only a short while to go heavily in debt by investing in luxurious transportation on the strength of one successful meeting. Needless to say, this young man long since has ceased to have any substantial place in the ministry. His reputation for extravagance, instability, and irresponsibility has preceded him wherever he goes. He owes bills to various persons which he probably will never pay. His wife lost confidence in him and left him. It appears that he belongs to that class of ministers who Paul said had made a shipwreck of their faith.

Let us give another example of a young man who was having unusual success in the ministry. His rise as an evangelist reached a climax in a southern town where large crowds attended his meetings. He arrived at the conclusion that God had called him to great things. He came to my office and during his visit manifested a spirit of extreme self-confidence. He gave me a rundown of his plans. Already he was gathering a large staff and was planning to set up an office. He would put out a magazine. He had ordered all sorts of equipment, a large tent with tractors, trucks, and all the paraphernalia to go with it. Indeed he was thoroughly convinced that God had singled him out as the man of the hour.

The more he talked the more disturbed I became. It seemed to me that I was witnessing a disaster in the making. I tried to caution him, but soon saw that nothing I said was getting through. However, his awakening was to come sooner than even I thought.

Intoxicated by his success he went deeper and deeper into debt. His next campaigns were not so profitable as the others. Inevitably he could not pay his bills as they came due. Debts were made some of which have never been paid to this day. This young man created for himself a bad image which has followed him ever since. What might have been a strong ministry today is practically shelved. All this trouble could have easily been avoided if he had kept a budget of his income and lived within it.

We could multiply cases like this of ministers who once had a bright future before them. But sudden success went to their head, and it was not long before they were in serious trouble. Although some learned their lesson and today are carrying on a sound ministry, others have never since recovered their stride.

THOSE WITH POOR ADVISORS

> "And the king answered the people roughly, and forsook the old men's counsel that they gave to him; And spake to them after the counsel of the young men, saying, My father made your yoke heavy, and I will add to your yoke: my father also chastised you with whips, but I will chastise you with scorpions" (I Kings 12:13-14).

Some ministers as a result of special gifts and talents attain an unusual prominence in the public eye. When a man achieves more than ordinarily usefulness in the ministry it may be necessary for him to engage a staff. The members of a man's staff usually wield a strong influence upon his way of thinking. Therefore, the selection of such personnel is most important. They must be men who are responsive to their leader's vision and calling, but not to his weaknesses.

We recall the case of one young evangelist who had unusual faith. There was no doubt that the gifts of healing were powerfully manifested in his ministry. In the short space of about eight months his meetings increased in size from filling local churches until he was ministering in the largest auditoriums in the land. The men who worked with him at that time were solicitous that with the enlargement of his ministry and influence he might continue to walk humbly before God and to recognize that it was the counsel and wisdom of others that played a large part in his success.

Nevertheless, with thousands of people attending his meetings, a coterie of followers who played to his vanity began to gather around him. They would flatter him and tell him that he was the greatest preacher in the world, that if he only had men who truly understood and appreciated his talents, he would be able to shake the country. Unfortunately, he fell for these flatteries and set up a new staff.

Under the momentum that had been built up, he continued to have outstanding meetings for some considerable time. But the result was inevitable. His ministry had crested. A slow decline was already beginning. These new men gave him poor advice. The result was that he began to make serious mistakes. Because of his secretive handling of finances and failures to keep his promises, he soon alienated many influential ministers. Misunderstandings followed. He no longer had the backing of churches he

118

previously enjoyed, and consequently his crowds fell off. Running into financial difficulties, he had to sell his equipment and suspend publication of his magazine. His staff who had been largely responsible for his downfall left him when he couldn't pay their salaries. Long since he passed into the limbo of forgotten men.

We recall another man who attained unusual prominence, not only in the Full Gospel world, but many denominational men received great inspiration from his ministry. His spiritual discernment was as perfect as anything that has ever come to our notice. Yet in the natural, his judgment was often that of a child. He was a humble man, but others not so humble and who were eager to shine by his reflected light gathered around this man of God. They had no other intention but to further their own interests. To make bad matters worse, some of his followers had some extremely weird ideas, a hodgepodge of teachings which were clearly unsound. They succeeded in publishing these errors under the name of the leader. Former intimates of this good man warned him of the dangers arising from the influence of those that surrounded him. Actually the purpose of those "friends" was to form a cult by using the leader's ministry. Mercifully the Lord removed the man from the scene so that his great work would not be lost.

The lesson is that a man must not only be sincere, but he must be careful about those whom he chooses to make his confidants. Rehoboam was not one of Judah's worst kings, and had he hearkened unto the counsel of the older men, he might have retained a united kingdom. Unfortunately, he chose to accept the counsel of men who were greedy for power and who were little interested in the welfare of the country. The result was revolution and disaster. Rehoboam's sad story has been repeated on a smaller scale many times in our day.

THOSE WHO BETRAY CONSCIENCE
WHEN THE PRICE IS HIGH ENOUGH

"Again, the devil taketh him up into an exceeding high mountain, and sheweth him all the kingdoms of the world, and the glory of them; and saith unto him, All these things will I give thee, if thou wilt fall down and worship me" (Matt. 4:8-9).

Satan knew that it was impossible to get Christ to yield to temptation for a small price. His only hope of subverting Him was to offer everything he had—"the kingdoms of this world." The devil was willing to step aside and let Christ take his place if He would but fall down and worship him. But if Satan had any such hopes, they were dashed to the earth by Christ's stern refusal of the offer.

Nevertheless, though Satan failed with Christ, he still believes that every man has his price. There is a story told of a certain individual who held an important position of trust in the government and had earned a reputation of high integrity. On a certain occasion he was approached by a lobbyist who operated on the principle that anyone could be bought if his price were met. This man offered the official $40,000 if he would exert his influence on the side of a certain bill that was coming up for a vote. The man indignantly refused the offer. The bribe was successively raised to $50,000 and then $60,000, but in each case it was refused. Finally the offer was raised to $80,000. With that the obnoxious visitor was unceremoniously ordered from the office with the words, "Now be gone. You are getting too near my price." The official meant by this that he was not going to dally with the temptation. It was dangerous to do so.

There is a strange thing about some men who are extremely conscientious in handling their ordinary financial obligations. They succeed in building for themselves an image of honesty and integrity. Yet when the great temptation comes, unsuspected ambition is often there to blind their judgment. They see what they think is a once-in-a-lifetime opportunity to advance themselves though it is at the expense of their honor and word.

Nevertheless, they will first rationalize their conduct. Not for a moment will they allow themselves to think they are doing wrong. It is human for men to justify their acts, however wrong. Even in the chaotic period of the Judges, we are told that "every man did that which was right in his own eyes." Most men who err will not violate their conscience; they alter it to bring it into conformity with their ambition. But like Jacob, there will be a time of reckoning—if not in this world then in the world to come. Men who do not "strive lawfully" for the prize, must miss it in the end.

It is sad to reflect that some men whom God has used in an outstanding way will violate their trust when they think the reward is great enough. These same individuals would have looked with horror on their act if it had involved only a small matter. Yet when the prize was of sufficient size, they were ready to forego their principles.

We have seen these things happen, and they are a warning to us of the limitations of men, even some who seem to be the soul of honor. For there is a Court of Last Resort which all of us must face eventually, and that is the judgement seat of Christ. There, all that is built on hay, wood, and stubble must be consumed in the fire (although they themselves will be saved as by fire) for the day will declare it.

THE TEMPTATION TO BUILD A SECT

Certain men have ability, or "charisma," as some call it to move men and attract followers far more than the average preacher. This ability spurs a dedicated man to become a great soul-winner. John Wesley is an example. Although his ministry rocked England for God, he had no desire to establish a kingdom of his own. He remained with the Church of England throughout his life. He had many opportunities to start an organization under his name, but he turned them all down. Looking backward, we can see that the time was well overdue for a new movement to arise distinct from the State Church. Although Wesley had nothing to do with its actual inception, shortly after his death the Methodist Church came into being.

But there are other men who are more ambitious than John Wesley. They are more interested in making a name than in giving themselves to the advancement of the work of the Lord. If such men would only keep their eye single unto God, thousands would rise up to call them blessed when their ministry was finished. Unfortunately, in many cases when a man discovers that he possesses unusual ability, he is tempted to try to build a kingdom for himself. In order to hold followers, he seeks some means to separate them from the mainstream of Scriptural revelation. This was the case of Jeroboam, who fearing the children of Israel would be lured back to allegiance to Rehoboam said to himself, "If this people go up to do sacrifice in the house of the Lord at Jerusalem, then shall the heart of this people turn again unto their Lord, even unto Rehoboam" (I Kings 12:27). So after taking counsel with idolatrous followers, he had two golden calves set up for the people to worship. This false worship became a curse both to him and to his people.

Today when men get the urge to set up a kingdom for themselves, they are likewise confronted with the problem of how to hold the loyalty of their followers. In almost all cases of the formation of a new sect, the leader makes himself believe he has discovered some overlooked truth of the Bible, which is of such world-shaking significance as to overshadow all else. Next he

121

proclaims that the church is willfully guilty of withholding this "great truth" from the people. This becomes a rallying point by which he can separate his followers from other believers. His work then in all respects becomes a sect, and if his teachings become sufficiently involved in error, the sect becomes a cult.

It is amazing the number of strange and unscriptural teachings that have emerged to divide the people of God. Often the doctrine emphasized involves a partial truth, but which in the main is unsound. In other instances the doctrine propagated is out-and-out error.

It is tragic to witness good people caught in the web of error and led astray by men who could have been of great service to the cause of Christ, but who because of ambition allow themselves to become leaders of sects or cults which at best can do nothing but further divide the body of Christ.

THE MESSIANIC COMPLEX

In line with the subject we have been discussing is that strange obsession we occasionally witness in leaders which is called the "Messianic complex." Leaders who are unusually successful will find Satan always on hand to tell them that they are God's man of the hour, that they are another Moses "to lead the church out of the wilderness" or that they are Elijah returned again.

A classic example which illustrates this is the life of Dr. John Alexander Dowie, whom God used to bring back apostolic ministry to the church at the turn of the century. The truth is that God used this man as few others to usher in His last day revival. In a few years' time he had gathered 100,000 followers, and his movement spread quickly around the world. The remarkable miracles of healing that occurred were of course what attracted the widespread interest and which made the movement so dynamic. A hostile municipal administration in Chicago tried to drive him from the city. During that time he was arrested nearly 100 times for "practicing medicine without a license." But in the end the administration itself was toppled from power, and a newspaper editor who had vilified Dowie went to the penitentiary for two years.

John Alexander Dowie had success in everything a minister of the gospel could desire. But he was not satisfied. He wanted new worlds to conquer. Ambition dominated him until it altered his personality. Satan played on his pride. A voice whispered, "Was not he, John Alexander Dowie, the great Elijah who was to come again? Was not he the First Apostle and also the Messenger of the Covenant spoken of by Malachi?" At first he rejected these suggestions, but gradually he began to believe them. In time he became a victim of these delusions. Assuming the title of "Messenger of the Covenant," he arrogated to himself an office that belonged to Christ. There could be only one conclusion to this sad story. He became like Nebuchadnezzar who said, "Is not this great Babylon that I have built for the house of the kingdom by the might of my power, and for the house of my majesty?" and then was struck down with madness and his kingdom taken from him. So John Alexander Dowie, a man who had done so much good, a man who had broken the fetters of ecclesiastical tradition that had bound the church for centuries, a man whom God greatly honored—yet because of his pride was struck down with an incurable disease, his kingdom going into receivership, and he himself dying a broken-hearted man.

There is no place in God's program today for those who have messianic complexes. God has only one man of the hour and that is our Lord Jesus Christ.

SOME LEADERS FAIL BECAUSE THEY "USE" PEOPLE FOR THEIR OWN ADVANCEMENT

There are some brilliant leaders who might attain to a high position in God's accounting, except that they insist on "using" people for their own advancement. How different was Christ who carefully trained His disciples that they might fit into positions of greater usefulness. To "use" people is a grave fault. Indeed such men apparently look upon themselves as so superior that they consider the interests of others to be inconsequential, therefore, to be given scant attention. The sin of Lucifer was his boundless ambition and disregard for God's interests. This evil of personal ambition is so serious that if not corrected, God must in the end bring low those affected by it. "He that exalteth himself shall be abased."

All of us owe something to others. Without the assistance of others the greatest among us would not go far. The least a leader can show to those who have helped him is his gratitude. Unfortunately, there are those who use the trust of others only as an opportunity to further their own personal interests and will ruthlessly set aside those who had helped them attain their present position without giving the matter a second thought.

123

Such methods may work for awhile. Apparently God will permit a man who does these things to prosper for a time. Indeed a part of his punishment may be that he is allowed to prosper in his delusion! For no man can hurt other members of the body of Christ with impunity. He who seeks to promote his own interest unfairly over those of other members of the body of Christ will ultimately be demoted and his works burned up as hay, wood, and stubble in the day of Christ.

In this world where often so little gratitude is manifested, it is refreshing to find some who do show it. It always gives new confidence to the people of God to learn that there are men whom God has especially used and who are interested in the welfare and advancement of others besides themselves. A beautiful illustration of this is found in the friendship of Jonathan and David. Jonathan knew that in God's providence David would supersede him. But even as his father Saul was insanely jealous of others, so Jonathan was the opposite; he was willing to see another honored before him. Although Jonathan sadly suffered because of a rebellious parent, God took full note of his generous spirit and allowed the beautiful story of his selflessness to be recorded in the Scriptures for all generations to see. With the exception of Christ Himself, Jonathan's life is the most wonderful illustration of true friendship in the Scriptures.

CHAPTER 20

Special Problems of Ministers

Ministers are constantly faced with questions involving money, morals, and ethics, some of which are not always easily answered. Sometimes under pressure, a preacher may do things or assent to them, which later he realizes were not altogether befitting an ambassador of Christ.

Generally speaking, most ministers desire to serve God and to live a life above reproach. In this chapter we shall note certain of these problems which are faced by ministers of the gospel. The following are some of the questions that have come to the writer's attention most frequently.

A MINISTER AND BUSINESS

QUESTION: What about a preacher's going into business?
ANSWER: There are no rules that will cover all circumstances, since life is too complex for that. A good general rule is that if a man is called to preach, he should stay by his calling. No man can be at his best if he is running a business and trying to preach at the same time. Still there are cases in which special circumstances need to be taken into consideration. Some ministers find their health failing, and their faith somehow has not enabled them to overcome this problem. There is the inevitable matter of support for their families, and they feel that the alternative is to turn to business.

There are those who upon going into the ministry find their congregations are too small to support their families. Even Paul was forced at times to work for a living.

Nevertheless, some preachers go into business for the purpose of making money in a big way, and they are soon completely absorbed in it. Usually their ministry suffers. Sometimes their business suffers also. They may find themselves failing in both enterprises. *If one throws himself entirely into the work of the*

125

ministry and exercises faith that God will supply his needs, he will usually find that his needs will be met, even though this may not be on a grand scale.

KEEPING A BUDGET

QUESTION: Should a preacher keep a budget?

ANSWER: By all means. The number of sad situations that occur in the ministry because ministers do not budget their income is alarming. These men do not intend to do wrong, but they involve themselves in obligations which the strength of their ministry does not warrant. Then they wake up to the cold reality and are tempted to do something desperate. Their actions not only become a reproach to the cause but they themselves may gain a reputation of undependability and dishonesty that will hinder their ministry from then on. We give one example which is a true case.

A certain young minister was having some outstanding meetings in which hundreds were being saved. Offerings were generous, and he became free and easy with his spending. Not accustomed to handling large sums of money, he began to write checks without due regard to how much he had in the bank. He did not keep a running balance in his check book. Apparently he did not know what a bank statement was. Consequently when his statement came that showed what his balance was several weeks previous, he assumed that that was the amount of money he actually still had. He wrote a number of checks far exceeding the real amount he now had in the bank. When the checks came back to the bank, they of course bounced. Soon the young man discovered he had run afoul of the law, and the county prosecutor talked of sending him to prison. He came into our office, almost in a state of hysteria, asking us to try to help him. We talked on the phone with the authorities and reasoned with them that the creditors were more likely to get their money if he stayed out of jail. They promised to suspend prosecution on the condition that he would make arrangements to repay systematically those to whom he had written bad checks. Somehow this minister was able to extricate himself from that situation, but he continued to get into financial difficulties. Eventually he got a reputation of undependability that has followed him ever since. All this trouble could have been avoided if he had kept a budget of his income and lived within it.

WILL FAILURE TO GIVE BRING A CURSE?

QUESTION: A certain minister in taking offerings told the

people that a curse would come upon them if they failed to give. Is this Scriptural?

ANSWER: It is very easy for reports to be exaggerated grossly. If a minister is not careful in his speaking, he may be reported as saying something different from what he really meant. It would seem that one would be very rash indeed to declare publicly that a curse would come upon people if they do not give him an offering.

People should give liberally to God's work only because they feel God would have them do so. They should give willingly and freely. "For God loveth a cheerful giver." They should always realize that giving to God is laying up treasures in heaven. Moreover, people should be taught to give in faith, believing that they shall receive in return, not for the purpose of hoarding up wealth, but so that they can give again and again. They should also feel free to give to the Lord as He leads them.

Certainly no minister should threaten anyone in order to make him give an offering. This would be grievously wrong. Nevertheless, the Bible teaches that "a curse" may come upon those who refuse to give God what is due Him (Malachi 3:8-10). There is such a thing as robbing God of what belongs to Him in tithes and offerings. And trouble may well come upon the person who knowingly is guilty of this sin. It may come in a variety of ways, through business losses, sickness, misfortunes, accidents, or poor crops. In other words, the blessing of God may be lifted from his life.

Though it is true that those who refuse to give to God what they owe to him commit a grave sin, *it is just as true that they must be perfectly free to give or not to give.* If a curse comes, it is God's prerogative to allow it to come. To attempt to secure a large offering by any such method mentioned above is wicked. To do so would be to follow in the way of Gehazi, whose heart was upon the silver of Naaman. He got the silver all right, but at the same time he got leprosy.

PRAYING FOR THOSE WHO GIVE A CERTAIN SUM

QUESTION: A minister calls for people to give a certain amount for an offering and then prays for only those who give the amount for which he asks. Is this right?

ANSWER: There is a possibility of danger here. It would not be wrong for a minister to pray for those who have given in sacrifice for the work of the Lord. Yet if only those who have money get prayed for, a serious misunderstanding could result.

The medieval church made a grave error by charging specific amounts for spiritual services. It finally reached a point at which it became a doctrine that a man's stay in purgatory could be shortened through payment of a certain amount. This error became a grievous sin in the sight of God. The poor and those who have little to give must always have equal opportunity to receive the spiritual ministry of the church.

Moreover, it would seem to be in very poor taste for a minister to be praying for people and taking money at the same time. Indeed it is nothing less than simony. Money handed to a minister while he is praying for the sick should be returned, graciously, of course. People must not associate that which was purchased by the blood of Christ with gold or silver. The gift of God cannot be obtained with money (Acts 8:20). Those who seek healing should give to God in the regular way as others do, according to their means. Indeed, to accept the blessing of God and to fail to do one's part to support the gospel would be the basest kind of ingratitude.

SCHEMES IN THE NAME OF RELIGION

QUESTION: In our city there is a preacher who has gone to elderly people and told them that God has revealed to him that they should deed their property over to him. He acquired several properties in that manner. Do you believe that God really told the minister to do that?

ANSWER: It sounds more like a confidence scheme, only in this case the operator used a religious cloak to get money. Jesus gave one of His severest denunciations against those who practiced such schemes. He said,

> "Woe unto you, scribes and Pharisees, hypocrites! for ye devour widows' houses, and for a pretence making long prayer: therefore ye shall receive the greater damnation" (Matt. 23:14).

In other words, the Pharisees, because they coveted wealth, went so far as to scheme to get the property of widows, even their homes, under religious pretense. Their long prayers apparently gave the widows the impression that they were very pious men and that God wanted them to handle their property. The inference is that these hypocrites swindled the widows out of their property, and used the proceeds for their own enrichment, instead of God's

128

work. Since there were hypocrites in Jesus' day, we need not be surprised if there are some of the same order today. Jesus said they will receive the greater damnation.

It should be understood that God does not speak against the widows' sacrificing for His work. He commended one widow for giving her last two mites. In the book of Acts we are told that some sold their houses and lands and brought the proceeds to the apostles' feet (Acts 4:32-34).

On occasions God may tell a person to sell certain of his property and give it to the cause of Christ. But if He does, He will speak to the individual and not require someone else to do it for Him.

CHAIN LETTER SCHEMES

QUESTION: A certain member of the church introduced a plan for getting money through a chain-letter system by which a letter was sent to ten people enclosing a list of names. Each person was requested to send a dollar to each name and in turn he would send out a list to ten others, dropping the top name and adding his. This plan was alleged to bring in a handsome return to each person on the list.

ANSWER: It is sadly true that such schemes have been introduced, even into the church, but they are nothing more nor less than a confidence game designed to transfer the dollars from the pockets of some to others. A few ministers have been involved in such schemes, and their actions are a disgrace to the ministry. The chain-letter produces nothing, and the man who schemes to get many dollars where he has put out little is nothing more than a confidence man. The U. S. government has designated all such schemes which involve the use of the mails as fraud, and the participants are in danger of a prison sentence. Although it is illegal to operate the "chain-letter" through the mails, conscienceless promoters, some under the guise of religion, still work similar methods outside the mails. Unfortunately, those looking for a way to get something for nothing continue to be their victims, including, sad to say, ministers.

A YOUNG MINISTER AND MARRIAGE

QUESTION: Should a young minister get married before he enters the active ministry?

ANSWER: Generally speaking it is wise for a young man to get his education and establish his ministry before he takes on the responsibility of a family. It is common knowledge that many a man who was called to the ministry became frustrated because of the financial problems involved.

Sometimes a young lady feels just as strong a call to the ministry as her fiance and is prepared to make sacrifices along with him. In some case her talents may exceed his. Then too, many preachers' wives have worked to help support their husbands, even while they were completing their education. This is certainly commendable, but not all women are willing to do this. Protracted financial difficulties can result in frustration and marital misunderstandings.

On the other hand, some ministers whose judgment is poor, sorely need a wife's counsel. If she has a ministry such as that of song leader, pianist, soloist, or altar worker, her presence in the meetings can be a definite asset.

There are some women who feel no calling to Christian service, yet they marry preachers. This is very unfortunate. If the minister's wife is a drone in the meetings, she is certain to draw adverse criticism. There is another important consideration. If she is the wife of an evangelist and becomes pregnant she will have to leave the field for a season. After the child is born she may find it too difficult or inconvenient to travel and have to remain at home. This presents complications. It may not be out of the way to note that some evangelists do not succeed in conducting themselves properly in the absence of their wives. Then too, long absences may cause a rift between them.

All these matters should be prayerfully considered before a person who has the call of God upon his life enters into matrimony. In most cases it is better to postpone marriage until one's ministry becomes established. It is certainly wise to take plenty of time to wait upon God in this important decision and make certain the right mate is chosen.

It is true of course that some successful ministers have married young and that many of their successes can be attributed to their choice of a wife.

THE PROBLEM OF A MINISTER'S CHILDREN

QUESTION: Why is it that a minister's children are so often a problem in the church?

ANSWER: Preachers' children are basically no better nor worse than other children in the church. But many factors operate to make their lives more difficult. They are often teased by thoughtless com-

130

panions and called "preacher," or "reverend," much to their annoyance.

Because they are preachers' children, they are ruthlessly thrown into the spotlight. Their faults are exposed to the public eye, and there is always someone ready to criticize them.

Moreover, in their peculiar position as children of the pastor, they inevitably become aware of the hypocrisies of other people including some ministers who make a profession but possess little. This circumstance tends to disillusion them about Christianity.

The fact that people expect more of them than other children and more than they are able to live up to tends to make them resentful. Actually, preachers' children are sinners and have to be born again just as any other children.

We recall the case of one of the most outstanding religious leaders of our time whose ministry has blessed multitudes. His church was in fact one of the largest in the world. Yet he had a son that caused him many a heartache and gave him no end of trouble. Finally, after one of the boy's worst escapades, he went to the elders of the church and told them that because he had failed to keep his son under subjection, he was no longer qualified to be their pastor. But the elders would not hear of his resignation, and stood by him nobly, telling him that they were going to share his burden by fasting and praying and believing God with him that the boy would be converted. Not long after, the young man was wonderfully saved and became a minister of the gospel.

One thing that is commonly overlooked is that Satan engages in a ruthless war against any minister who is being especially used by God. When the devil perceives he can make little headway against the man himself, he will often attack him through his family. Many a good man has been broken in that way. The church owes it to the pastor to hold up his hands and help him to pray through for his children.

Even though the children of ministers sometimes go through some rough times, on the whole, after they are grown, they rank at the very top among the citizens of the nation.

WHAT ABOUT WOMEN'S ATTIRE?

QUESTION: What should a pastor say and do in the matter of women's attire?

ANSWER: Some ministers have gained a reputation as "clothesline" preachers, who in nearly every sermon make some allusion to women's dress, usually in the negative. It is doubtful that anything is gained by continual harping on the subject. Nevertheless, the Scriptures do have something to say on the matter of women's dress. The apostle Peter, when referring to this subject said, "Whose adorning let it not be that outward adorning of plaiting the hair, and of wearing of gold, or of putting on apparel, but let it be the hidden man of the heart in that which is not corruptible even the ornament of a meek and quiet spirit, which is in the sight of God of great price" (I Pet. 3:3-4). Obviously what this means is not that women should not give attention to their personal appearance, but that they should avoid the extremes of fashion, especially those that lean to immodesty. Paul bears this out in I Timothy 2:9-10.

Christians cannot help but be concerned over certain trends in women's dress which in recent years have passed the point of decency. It appears that Satan is deliberately attempting to make nudity acceptable to the public. Restaurants by the scores employ "topless" waitresses. Designers have offered "topless" bathing suits for women, although up until the present time municipal ordinances have in most areas prohibited their use. Nevertheless, bathing suits have been reduced in size to the point of indecency. National advertising portrays the unclad, or almost unclad female as a standard method of selling their products. The motion picture code now permits absolute nakedness on the screen. Models completely nude shamelessly pose before mixed art classes in colleges.

The emphasis continually is on sex appeal, the result of which is tending to national promiscuity and with it a weakening of the foundations of society.

The latest fad is the miniskirt which in the judgment of many officials abroad is obscene and in some countries actually prohibited. That Satan is back of this trend to nudity cannot be denied.

The demon-possessed man in the tombs would wear no clothing. But when he was delivered from the evil powers, the first thing he did was to put on clothes.

A generation ago, people who frequented nudist clubs were considered perverts and oddballs. Exhibitionists when caught were sent to prison. But now near-nudity is becoming the fashion and pressure is on for public acceptance of complete nudity. Certainly the minister of the gospel must raise his voice in strong protest against this vicious evil. Christian women should resent and resist this sex-exploitation that is seeking the degradation of womanhood.

RELIGIOUS SCAVENGING

QUESTION: A writer in a certain periodical wrote a scurrilous series of articles against the deliverance ministry, giving the impression that all who were in this ministry were interested only in getting the people's money. He especially attacked the man for whom he had worked previously. He claimed that God told him to expose those that were not doing right. (It may be noted that this man died shortly after he wrote these articles.)

ANSWER: The implication that all men who pray for the sick are crooked is more than mischievous; it is wicked and libelous. It is a direct slur upon Christ who practiced divine healing. There are many ministers who pray for the sick that are conscientious and careful in the handling of their finances.

Granted, it is true that there are some unscrupulous men in this ministry. Jesus had one in the apostolic group—Judas Iscariot. That being so, we must recognize that there will be those in the ministry today that give way to temptation. It is something which all denominations have to face. When we find a minister who is deliberately dishonest in his dealings, it should be no cause for surprise, but it should call forth our pity and prayers for the one who has chosen a sure road to disaster.

We do not believe God calls His ministers to be spiritual scavengers. Any man who delights in digging up all the dirty linen he can and waving it before the public is a sick man. He does himself no good nor does he do the church a service. We of course refer not to preaching against evil which is the responsibility of every minister, but rather to the practice of attacking personalities which only invites recriminations.

We do believe it shows a poor spirit for a man to accept support from another minister over a period of years, and then finally when he leaves pours out his venom against him.

We recall the case of a minister some years ago who had once been a convict, but God saved him and gave him a fruitful ministry. Later he and another minister became side-tracked into printing a scandal sheet. All the mistakes and short-comings of prominent ministers were gathered up and eagerly splashed into print. Naturally the time comes, sooner or later, when those who traffic in this trade get hold of some item which is untrue or at least cannot be proven. A woman minister who was attacked by these men sued for libel, and a court awarded a heavy judgment. When the convicted publishers could not pay, they were sentenced to a month in the county jail. Another minister and I visited the pair. They sustained their wounded ego by making themselves believe that they were suffering for a worthy cause like Paul and Silas. They only deluded themselves. Neither man was ever effective in the ministry again. Not long after, one of these men was killed in an air accident.

We need not busy ourselves to expose the unsavory acts of those who make mistakes in the ministry. The devil who is the accuser of the brethren has plenty of willing messengers who will gladly perform the task.

SHOULD A CHRISTIAN DRINK ALCOHOL?

QUESTION: What about a Christian's drinking alcohol? Many Christians in other countries drink alcohol as a matter of custom and think nothing about it. In defense of their position, they claim that Jesus turned the water into wine at a marriage festival; therefore, He sanctioned its use.

ANSWER: Perhaps there is no error more widely held than the idea that there is only one kind of wine—alcoholic wine. Yet if people would only go to the dictionary, they would find that there are two kinds—fermented and *unfermented.* Funk and Wagnall's *College Standard Dictionary* says that wine is "the expressed juice of grape, fermented or unfermented." Webster's *New Collegiate Dictionary* says, "The fermented or loosely the unfermented juice of any fruit used as a beverage." There are two kinds of wine just as there are both hard cider and sweet cider. To fail to make this distinction can result in a most dangerous error. Just as the dictionary declares that there are two kinds of wine, the Bible also makes it clear that are are two kinds—fermented and unfermented. For example, Daniel the prophet refused the king's alcoholic wine (Dan. 1:8). But he drank another kind, except when he was fasting (Dan. 10:2-3). Obviously he drank unfermented wine, or the two passages would be contradictory.

Christ turned water into wine at the marriage feast. But fresh wine is always non-alcoholic. Wine has to stand a length of time before it ferments. Bread, when kept a length of time, becomes moldy. When Christ multiplied the loaves and fishes to feed the multitudes, did He create moldy bread or rotten fish? Did He create fermented wine at the marriage feast? The answer in both cases is, of course, no.

The evidence in the New Testament that there were two kinds of wine, fermented and unfermented, is irrefutable. Luke 5:37-39 says as follows:

> "And no man putteth new wine into old bottles; else the new wine will burst the bottles, and be spilled, and the bottles shall perish. But new wine must be put into new bottles; and both are preserved."

The new wine was obviously unfermented, since it must be put in new bottles. The old wineskins were full of fermenting lees which would quickly speed up the process of fermentation of the new wine, thus bursting the bottles. Failure to make this obvious distinction between alcoholic and non-alcoholic wine has led to tragedy in the lives of many people, even some ministers.

God shows us what can happen when a believer drinks, by recording two instances in the Old Testament. The first was that of Noah who became drunk on wine. This led to his making a spectacle of himself. He became an object of derision to his irreverent son Ham, who by his wicked act brought a curse upon his descendants (Gen. 9:18-27). The second case was that of Lot. His use of wine finally resulted in his daughters' committing incest with him (Gen. 19:30-38).

That either ministers or Christian laymen should become addicted to alcohol is unthinkable. God's instructions to the Nazarites who were especially called of God were not to drink wine nor strong drink. The book of Proverbs is full of warnings against the use of alcohol (Prov. 20:1; 23:29-32; Hab. 2:5).

In the Old Testament those who went in to minister at the altar *were forbidden to drink wine or strong drink.*

> "Do not drink wine nor strong drink, thou, nor thy sons with thee, when ye go into the tabernacle of the congregation, lest ye die: it shall be a statute for ever throughout your generations: And that ye may put difference between holy and unholy, and between unclean and clean" (Lev. 10:9,10).

Did Christ violate this command by creating and drinking alcoholic beverages? If so then according to the above Scripture He made that which is unholy and unclean. Let a man consider this solemnly before he makes such a charge against Christ.

SHOWMANSHIP IN THE PULPIT

QUESTION: What about ministers who resort to showmanship in the pulpit in order to attract attention?

ANSWER: First, we should define what we mean by showmanship. If a minister demonstrates the power of God through manifestation of the healing power of God, he is fulfilling the Bible pattern. If that is showmanship, then Christ Himself used it. The apostle Paul said that he "came not with excellency of speech, or of wisdom, declaring unto you the testimony of God . . . and my speech and my preaching was not with the enticing words of man's wisdom, but in the demonstration of the spirit and power" (I Cor. 2:1, 4).

On the other hand, a certain dignity is required of an ambassador of Christ. The man who acts like a clown or turns the pulpit into a vaudeville stage is degrading the ministry. There is no place for buffoonery in preaching the Word of God. The minister should never lend himself to stunt marriages, mock funerals, or any other conduct that is unbecoming to the ministry. Gimmicks and gadgets do not help the cause of Christ.

We recall an instance in which the pastor of a church raised money for an evangelist by having people pin dollar bills to his clothes. Only sheer ignorance would permit a minister to resort to such crude tactics. He perhaps saw someone else use this method and thoughtlessly followed suit. Such acts can only result in degrading the evangelist and pastor in the eyes of intelligent people.

WHAT ABOUT THE THEATER?

QUESTION: What about a minister's attending the theater?
ANSWER: First of all let us distinguish between the principle of the motion picture and the theater itself. Certainly the invention itself is neither good nor bad any more than the art of printing is good or bad. A film can carry an inspiring message, or it can be a medium to encourage violence or inflame the passions of people. The screen merely reflects what is shown on it, be it good or bad, just as a book may be a vehicle of good or evil.

But the question of the theater and quality of the films which are shown in this institution is another matter altogether. Let us consider this question by noting the words of John Crosby, noted writer for a syndicated column, who speaks not for the church, but on behalf of common decency. In this article in the *Saturday Evening Post* (Nov. 10, 1962) entitled "Movies Are Too Dirty," he gives a scathing indictment and denunciation of the pictures generally produced by the movie industry. He says:

"I can't pinpoint the precise moment in history when I became aware that I was tired of dirty movies, but I suspect it came somewhere in the middle of *Walk on the Wild Side.* I fell asleep is what I did. It was some point after the pimp had beaten up his prostitute in the bordello and some point before the lesbian madam tried to pin the Mann Act on the fellow who loved her girl friend . . . In the enormous city of New York with scores of movies to choose from, there is hardly a single one fit to show a girl of that age (thirteen). In fact, I'm afraid Maggie has seen a lot of movies that I don't approve of her seeing, because—well, how do you know in advance? . . . Take *Cape Fear* which may be the most sordid, vicious, and utterly depraved movie I have ever seen . . . I must confess the rape scene in *The Virgin Spring* made me physically sick . . . the girl is of such dazzling purity and innocence that her desecration and murder are almost the outermost limit of evil."

Jack Webb, originator of "Dragnet" on television, in his best seller *The Badge* describes the eccentricities and excesses of Hollywood in terms that make one shudder. He describes the antics of the stars, of their parties, wild drinking, dope orgies, scandals, sex escapades that make a decent person recoil with horror. And he is in a position as few are, to know the real truth about Hollywood.

There are persons who claim that ministers opposing the theater are extremists who are puritanical and narrow in their ways. But Billy Graham, who is widely recognized as an authority by millions of people in his syndicated column on May 6, 1963 has this to say about the movies:

> "*Question: Is it wrong to allow my daughter to go to the movies?*
>
> *Answer:* "I must answer you by asking, 'What kind of movies?' There are many wholesome and inspirational films being made and exhibited by church organizations. I can wholeheartedly recommend these. Though limited in budget, it is the intention of the producers of these films to instruct, to inspire, and to reform. Many of the secular films, such as most of Walt Disney's productions, are also wholesome.
>
> "However, I can say without qualification that it is not only wrong but sinful to expose your daughter to some of the filth that is being exhibited on the modern motion picture screen."

He then quotes John Crosby, the noted columnist as saying,

"I violently object to young teens' being exposed to this sort of thing, because it plants in them the idea that sexuality is essentially a degenerate, shameful, rather frightening thing, instead of the joyful, natural God-given urge that it is." And Billy Graham continues:

> "Severe censorship in a free society seems to be taboo. The place to stop this sort of thing is at the box office. When decent people stop attending indecent films, the producers won't have any incentive in making them.
> "The Bible teaches: 'Come out from among them and be ye separate saith the Lord and touch not the unclean thing, and I will receive you.'"

Again Billy Graham speaking in the First Baptist Church in Dallas, Texas, on January 22, 1967, said:

> "As for the movies, sex has become the god of the American people. They can scarcely have a movie today without a sex scene. They have gotten beyond nudity. They want to have sex orgies. And the producers say that since they want it, they are going to be given it. When those sex scenes come on the screen, everyone in the theater becomes quiet. You can hear a whisper. It is as if people were sitting around a communion table. Sex has become the god of the American people."

This is Billy Graham's statement on movies, and he speaks for a larger section of evangelical Christianity than perhaps any other man.

The theater has long had a reputation as being a worldly place. Movie attendance, therefore, jeopardizes a Christian's testimony. How could it be otherwise? What do we see at the front of the foyer of a movie theater? We see the gaudy billings of men and women displayed in various states of semi-nudity, and often in compromising situations. It is not unusual that the announcement with the billing includes a statement that the current showing is a daring expose' of some moral deviation guaranteed to shock the viewers. Those who attempt to defend the purity of Hollywood pictures are contradicting what the purveyors of the films themselves claim for them. The movie house proprietors certainly do not want the theater-going crowd to think their films are clean, for they know that a debased public taste does not go for clean movies. Even so-called good films often have something salacious or suggestive somewhere in it to make it a box office attraction.

It is significant to note that worldy people are often the ones most shocked when they find Christians attending the movies. They are not deceived about their real character.

A FINAL ADMONITION

QUESTION: In a few words what do you consider the best advice to give to a young man who is just entering the ministry?
ANSWER: "Commit thy way unto the Lord; trust also in him; and he shall bring it to pass." Psa. 37:5)

I would say that the most important advice that I could give a young minister is that he make a complete committal to God. There are four committals that every minister should make. The first is the committal of his soul. Of this Paul the apostle could say, "I know whom I have believed, and am persuaded that he is able to keep that which I have committed unto him against that day" (II Tim. 1:12). Many commit themselves to God, but with reservations. There must be no reservations. The committal must be total; it must be irrevocable. And why not? One minute after the heart ceases to beat and the spirit leaves the body, we shall be utterly dependent upon God's mercy and the integrity of His promise. Since our commitment to God must be a total one then, why not let it be so now?

The second committal should be that of our body. Not the committal of the body at the graveside, which is read in a memorial service, but the committal of our body while we are alive. The apostle speaks of this in I Thes. 5:23: "And the very God of peace sanctify you wholly; and I pray God your whole spirit and soul and body be preserved blameless unto the coming of our Lord Jesus Christ." God's plan for his saints is that they should be preserved blameless, body, soul, and spirit as long as they live on this earth. A body that has a disease such as cancer, tuberculosis, or crippling arthritis can scarcely be said to be preserved. Repeated sicknesses and healings are not the answer. The covenant of healing that God gave to His people was *immunity from disease* (Exod. 15:25-26). This promise was repeated in Exodus 23:25 and Deut. 7:15, "I will take sickness from the midst of thee." But all these promises of God must be claimed. There must be a definite act of committal of our bodies to God. Satan will challenge our act. He will not let us enter into that sphere of dominion without a struggle. *But his power is limited, and there can only be one result if we stand our ground, and that is, total victory. The minister should not limit this com-*

mittal to his own body, but he should claim divine health for his entire family.

Third, there should be the committal of our material needs to God. Neither riches nor poverty should be regarded as a sign of God's favor. Too much riches can destroy. Nevertheless, if all Christians were poor, who would support the evangelization of the world? There will be testing times for God's people. But after the test there should be deliverance. God will deliver His people from poverty. As the psalmist said, "I have not seen the righteous forsaken, nor his seed begging bread" (Psa. 37:25). And John the Beloved wrote in his final epistle, "Beloved, I wish above all things that thou mayest prosper and be in health, even as thy soul prospereth" (III John 2).

Fourth, commit your children into the hands of God. Ministers do not escape the common trial of children growing up and tending to wander from the fold of God. It is a humbling experience that after the minister has preached to others on how to rear children, he finds a rebellious spirit developing among his own offspring. But God knows all about these things. He wants the minister and his wife to commit their children into His hands. He has the resources and knows exactly how to apply pressure and how to bring each member of the family into the place of submission to Him. As the apostle said to the Philippian jailer, ". . . Believe on the Lord Jesus Christ, and thou shalt be saved, and thy house" (Acts 16:31).

And so it is that God is calling his ministers into a place of total committal to Him. It is none other than the secret place of the Most High. There the man of God will "abide under the shadow of the Almighty . . . A thousand shall fall at thy side, ten thousand at thy right hand, but it shall not come nigh thee . . ."

Gifts.

Free gifts to every willing believer, power to live victoriously in the closing evil days of this age. Study the Holy Spirit—His character, His purpose, His gifts—through the careful writings of Gordon Lindsay. His thoughts on the baptism of the Holy Spirit, the gifts of the Spirit and the current controversy of their use in the Church have become modern classics. Important reading for every full-gospel teacher and layman.

$2.50 EACH
Complete set of 4—$9.00
Prices subject to change without notice. Please include
$.75 each or $1.50 for the set for postage & handling.

**Order from
Christ For The Nations • P.O. Box 24910 • Dallas, TX 75224**

Jerusalem. While thousands of Jews gather in this ancient capital city to celebrate the feasts of Passover and Pentecost, 120 timid, frightened followers of Christ huddle in a tiny second-story chamber to seek a promised boldness their resurrected Lord had commissioned almost 10 days before.

The afternoon is dusty and hot. Then, a quiet stirring, a moving power permeates the upper room! The Holy Spirit!

Follow the story of that first outpouring of the Holy Spirit and the miraculous years that followed through the eyes of one of America's most prolific authorities on the subject, Gordon Lindsay. The events of the day of Pentecost, the communal Church, the conversion of Paul and the advance of the gospel into Europe and Asia are but a few of his topics you won't want to miss. **Acts in Action,** five concise, easy-to-study commentaries on The Acts of The Apostles. **Order your complete set today!**

ACTS IN ACTION

ORDER FROM:
Christ For The Nations
P.O. Box 24910
Dallas, TX 75224

$1.25 each or $5.00 a complete set
plus postage & handling
Prices subject to change without notice

Postage & Handling
Up to $3.00.............. $ .75
$3.01 to $15.00.......... $1.50
$15.01 to $25.00......... $2.50
Sorry No C.O.D.'s or Stamps